This book is genius. Excelling at yo involves more than just hard work anu possessing strong technical skills. In *Leading Beyond the Numbers*, the author delves into the additional aspects that I now regret not learning about earlier in my career. Susan provides a clear and understandable explanation of complex concepts and shares perspectives and stories that can improve your productivity, performance, and overall wellbeing. I will be encouraging my whole team to read this book.

John Barrett, CFO Global Operations
and Supply Chain, *Medtronic*

At a time when the world seems obsessed with the impacts on business and society of Artificial Intelligence (AI), along comes a book which reminds us of just how important it is to be human. *Leading Beyond the Numbers* is a fascinating and informative book which advocates the latent potential of escaping the linear mind and tapping into the broader intelligence of our emotions and our bodies. It seems to relish the juxtaposition that it is written by career accountant and the wit and tone of the book also challenge the traditional sterntypes of this noble profession. With this timely and enjoyable book, Susan Ní Chríodáin makes a strong case for why we must urgently get more balance into the emotional balance sheet of corporations.

Gib Bulloch, Author, *The Intrapreneur,*
Founder and CEO, *The Craigberoch Business Decelerator*

If you're a results-focused leader, you need to read this book. Susan Ní Chríodáin has used her lived experience to devise a roadmap for measuring the unmeasurable: How do we look beyond the numbers and account for our emotions at work? How do we become more human at work because our people are our greatest asset? Susan has the answers, and they're in this book.

Aoife O'Brien, Founder of *Happier at Work* and host of the *Happier at Work podcast*

It's accountancy, *Jim*, but not as we know it! What a great book. Susan Ní Chríodáin neatly summarizes insights from current understandings of stress, emotion and neuroscience research and makes them deeply relevant to the workplace. She knows her audience well. The reframing of business phrases, to make them relevant to the process of regulation of feelings, is cleverly done and made me smile a number of times. She is remarkably successful in explaining complex concepts in simple, meaningful ways. Read this book to understand how your performance at work can be improved by knowing the habits of how your brain and body try to protect you in the modern workplace. In fact, read this book to be happier and more effective in all areas of life, not just in business.

Steve Haines, Author of *Really Strange* books and Director of *Body College*

By considering and valuing the power of emotions in the workplace, Susan Ní Chríodáin, a former finance director, shows she is unwilling to be siloed or to 'stay in her lane', and we are all better for it. In a uniquely convincing yet 'non-pushy' style, she implores the reader to take a deeper and more holistic view of themselves and reveals how a more mindful approach to emotions can make a difference in our lives and relationships. Reading the remarkably human *Leading Beyond the Numbers*, I was surprised to find how much the book challenged me to reflect and reconsider so many things about myself, both personally and professionally. As a Founder and former CEO of a large company in Africa, this book helped reveal the significance that emotions played in both our company's challenges and our successes. I would encourage leaders and leadership teams of all types to make use of the wisdom shared in this inspirational book.

Kevin Ashley, Co-Founder and former CEO,
Java House Africa

In a world driven by technology and algorithms *Leading Beyond the Numbers* is a compelling call to account for our humanity and to develop greater self-awareness. Through insightful parallels between emotional balance and financial prudence this book bridges the gap between personal well-being and corporate success and performance. It is a guidebook that unveils the relationship between managing our emotions and balancing our 'inner books' and the importance of fostering a culture of empathy in both personal and professional spheres. It's a must-read for those seeking a holistic approach to success, reminding us that a thriving society and corporate environment depend not just on numbers but on our collective emotional wealth.

Charlotte Cadoux, VP of Human Resources, *Aptissen SA*

Leading Beyond the Numbers explains how and why leaders need to reintroduce humanity into business by getting out of our heads and into our bodies. This isn't another WooWoo rant though, it's a down-to-earth guide, from an accomplished storyteller and former finance director, grounded in science and as inspiring as a *TED Talk*.

Alexander Inchbald, Climate artist, bestselling author, Founder of #Masterpiece Movement

I've just finished Susan Ní Chríodáin's book and I'm glad I took the time to read it. This topic needs more attention and understanding from both aspiring and well-established leaders at all levels. Understanding how our own human nature and that of others interrelate can make a huge difference in people performance and ultimately business performance. *Leading Beyond the Numbers* is a really good read, thought provoking, challenging and inspiring all at the same time.

Kevin Chevis, Former Executive Vice President, *Jenoptik*

Through facts, quotes, stories, and, yes, numbers, you will find yourself reflecting about life and purpose. More than once, while reading *Leading Beyond the Numbers*, I had to stop and reflect – this book is a true gift!

Diego Adame, Senior Director, *The LEGO Foundation*

Susan Ní Chríodáin tackles the question of how to put more of ourselves into our work with aplomb. This well-researched book delves into the practical, personal, and philosophical aspects of true leadership. But you won't just think differently after reading *Leading Beyond the Numbers* – you'll feel a sense of expansion.

Greta Solomon, Freelance journalist
and author of *Heart, Sass & Soul*

Leading Beyond the Numbers is a triumph – a must-read for all leaders. I could not put it down and made copious notes. Susan has weaved together her personal experience from workplaces, insights from her podcast interviews and the nuggets of wisdom from the thought leaders in emotional and somatic intelligence in a very compelling, clear and concise way. This book is like a lighthouse in a sometimes-overwhelming sea of information, it lights a pathway for us, the reader, to reflect, question, build self-insight and begin to make changes that are worth making, to make us better leaders. I love Susan's practical, human approach which ignites new possibilities in the human soul.

Kerry Cullen, Somatic Coach,
Facilitator and Chartered Psychologist

Leading Beyond the Numbers is a compelling exploration of the importance and value of emotions in business. Susan thoughtfully challenges the notion that to be professional one has to suppress emotions and instead advocates for both reason and emotions. In a world where business leaders often struggle to optimise employee engagement and employees likewise struggle to find fulfilment Susan provides original and thought-provoking insights to fill the gap. A must read.

Simon Moore, Author, Partner,
Adams & Moore Solicitors LLP

Leading Beyond the Numbers is such an important book that should be required reading for everyone starting their first job. It provides valuable insights into how our brain and body work and the impact of sleep, stress, change, food, and exercise on our performance and ability to engage at work. The personal stories shared illustrate the importance of meaning and sensemaking in organizations as well as the importance of compassion and taking time to feel and describe *all* our emotions. The case the author makes for bringing our whole selves to work and the need for organizations to recognize the whole person at work is essential knowledge for any leader or manager.

Dr Susanne Evans, Founder,
Feldspar Consulting Ltd. and Podcaster, *ChangeStories*

In *Leading Beyond the Numbers,* I can hear the intensity of Susan's voice in every page as she captures that conundrum on whether numbers can, at the same time, be factual and emotional. To succeed as an author, you need to leave your reader with something that they will carry forward with them into their future and I am stirred by a miniscule thing; one part of a sentence: 'These terms, debit and credit, both come from Latin and mean to owe and to believe.' This, for me, is the crux; a debtor, factually, owes me but a creditor, in handing me goods without payment, has shown belief in me. I can think of no better example of *Leading Beyond the Numbers* than this.

John Shinnick, Portfolio Non-Executive Director

Such a creative and different approach to wellbeing in the workplace. I love how the author uses her extensive background in accounting to tie this essential topic (often deemed to be a bit 'fluffy') into the company accounts and therefore financial health and performance – something that matters to many leaders! It's also very well researched and has definitely encouraged me to think differently about how I approach life. Fantastic food for thought for managers and leaders of all organizations. As mental health and wellbeing continue to gallop up the company agenda, is this a book you can afford *not* to read?

Andi Lonnen, FCCA, *FBP Academy*, author of
Introduction to Finance Business
Partnering & Be Fabulous at Finance!

Accounting, and particularly management accounting, is as much about people as it is about numbers – telling the story of the business and the decisions it has made. Understanding the idiosyncrasies that make us human can help leaders tell their business story in a far more authentic, compelling way. But *Leading Beyond the Numbers* is not a book about accountancy, or leadership, or neuroscience. It is a fascinating exploration of all three, in which Susan applies familiar accounting and not-so-familiar neuroscience concepts to the world of work, and the people within it. Her engaging, relatable style and boundless curiosity make this an inspiring and thought-provoking read. Ultimately, our influence as leaders and finance professionals is determined by the mindset we choose to adopt. This book may very well change yours.

Rebecca McCaffry CPFA, FCMA, CGMA, Associate
Technical Director, *Chartered Institute*
of Management Accountants (CIMA)

In *Leading Beyond the Numbers*, Susan Ní Chríodáin, with her rich background in accounting and finance, reimagines the future of work. She expertly illustrates how accounting for our feelings and integrating emotional intelligence into the fabric of our professional lives can revolutionize our decision-making and perception of workplace culture. This book is a vital guide for anyone looking to navigate and shape the evolving landscape of work where numbers tell only part of the story.

Andrew Codd, FCMA CGMA MBA, author of *The Audacious Finance Partner* & *The Finance Mentors' Ledger*

Leading Beyond the Numbers is a unique and thought-provoking book of experiences and intuitive ideas about how we can make the workplace truly productive. Conveyed through the prism of accounting, Susan superbly articulates how we can better address some of those tricky and sometimes painful issues at work while supporting others – all in all, bringing out the best of ourselves.

Gabriella McMichael, PhD, United Nations *World Food Programme*

Susan takes us on a wonderful journey through her past and by doing so, provides insight into all of our futures and asks us to consider who we really are at work. A captivating and thoughtful look at what it means to balance the books of our lives – our bodies, minds, hearts, and environment to determine what it means to be human. With stories, humour, and anecdotes, Susan uses her life in finance and *beyond* to ask the Big Questions about life itself.

Ellen Leith, Founder, *The Purchase to Pay Network (PPN)*

I know from working with Susan for many years that she fully vests herself in what she does. That is what makes this book so valuable. This is lived experience, years of learning, humour, and heartfelt perspectives on how life and work are not separate things, but how they can and should reinforce each other. Businesses almost always say that their people are their greatest asset, but too rarely treat them as such. In what feels like a more complex and uncertain world, leaders need to nurture this human capital and allow us all to support one another by turning up at work as ourselves, *not just* as staff. *Leading Beyond the Numbers* brings together data (numbers), science, and experience in an inspiring narrative that will have you reflecting on your own work-life.

John Fairhurst, Head, Private Sector Engagement, *The Global Fund to Fight AIDS, Tuberculosis and Malaria*

Through a unique lens *Leading Beyond the Numbers* offers compelling insights into our work-lives that resonate with profound meaning. A must-read for aspiring leaders seeking fresh perspectives and a deeper understanding of their impact.

Deirdre de Bhailís, General Manager, *Dingle Hub*

LEADING BEYOND THE NUMBERS

How accounting for emotions
...tips the balance at work

Susan Ní Chríodáin

First published in Great Britain by Practical Inspiration Publishing, 2024

ISBN   978-1-78860-586-1   (hardback)
        978-1-78860-510-6   (paperback)
        978-1-78860-512-0   (epub)
        978-1-78860-511-3   (mobi)

Want to bulk-buy copies of this book for your team and colleagues? We can customize the content and co-brand *Leading Beyond the Numbers* to suit your business's needs.

Please email info@practicalinspiration.com for more details.

Practical Inspiration
Publishing

Dedication

For Rae, Alvy, Markéta and Cosmo with all my love.
And for everyone reshaping the future of work
and workplaces, this book is dedicated to your expansive
vision and pursuit of fulfilment.

Contents

Foreword

The origins of accounting

Estimates vary, but it is thought some of the earliest recorded financial accounts are from ancient Egyptian tablets from circa 3300BC. These accountancy practices predated money and would have recorded an inventory of goods kept in royal premises.

These early forms of accountancy then expanded into areas such as Greece and Rome via trading routes.

Human beings for over 5,000 years have been recording financial information. As the old saying goes you measure what you treasure and for a large bulk of human civilization that has been profit, loss and how many donkeys you might have in the stable.

For millennia we have been asking ourselves:

- How much does this cost?
- How much stock do we have?
- When do we run out of gold?

The data science revolution

Fast forward to the 1900s and business becomes a process of profit, loss, revenue overheads and balance sheets.

As business evolved so did the practice of marketing. Today a modern marketing team includes creatives, social media managers, AI experts, sociologists and data scientists.

I spent the first 10 years of my career working in the data of marketing and in my opinion the way companies use behavioural and data science to encourage people to buy their stuff, is about 10 years ahead of the way we use data and science to create workplaces where employees can thrive.

Companies are prepared to speculate to accumulate in their sales and marketing but are more hesitant to make the same investments in their people. As Susan pointed out to me, many organizations simply see their people as a 'cost'. Therefore any new spend on a company's biggest 'cost centre' needs a business case.

A business case for the new HR system, a business case for dismantling systemic racism, a business case for happiness. The list goes on.

Flip the question

What I find odd is we never need to make a business case for traditional ways of doing things.

CEOs are often asked to make the business case for happiness, hybrid working patterns, mental health awareness, wellbeing programs and diversity and inclusion (D&I) initiatives.

There is data and research to make these cases but the opposite questions and data should also be asked, for example:

- What is the business case for unhappiness?
- What is the business case for a 5-day work week?
- What is the business case for mandating for everyone to return to the office?

- What is the business case for only recruiting from a narrow select group of people all from the same background?

A lot of what happens at work occurs because: 'That is the way it has always been done around here', or even worse, 'This is standard practice in this industry, that is how everyone does it'.

So much has changed over the last 5,000 years but at the same time so much has stayed the same.

5,000 years later... in Ipswich, England

To me growing up, Cartouche was a nightclub in Ipswich.

Today we know that in ancient Egypt there were cartouches that featured hieroglyphic symbols that signified global universal needs such as health, life and happiness.

For example, the Eye of Horus is thought to be a healing symbol. There were also symbols that represented health, life and happiness. Other examples include the lotus flower, symbolizing rebirth and rejuvenation.

So not only were the ancient Egyptians accounting for their belongings, they were also sharing emotions and how they felt through symbols.

So you could argue that the ancient Egyptians taught us accounting and recording the importance of emotions.

But why has it taken us 5,000 years to consider linking them?

Profit and loss 2.0

First, one of the main barriers to joining up the dots has been technology but that is no longer an excuse. We have all the data, AI and computing power to change how we account.

We now have the technology but accountancy practices won't change until there is a huge mindset shift.

I am seeing more and more of our customers at The Happiness Index feed the emotional data that they get from our platform into their profit and loss (P&L).

Most financial data looks backwards. However, emotional data is a predictor of the future. It can help leaders understand not just the financial health of an organization but now we can look at the cultural health of an organization.

I refer to this as the 'P&L 2.0 revolution'. I see it as a form of emotional intelligence at scale that helps an organization improve its decision making.

Now that I have set the scene I will hand over to Susan to go beyond the numbers and consider what is possible.

Matt Phelan
www.mattphelan.co.uk
Co-founder, The Happiness Index
December 2023

Introduction

For centuries a battle has raged between emotion and reason, leading us to value thinking over feeling and brain over body. That has resulted in many of us relying on and developing our cognitive intelligence whilst diminishing our capacity to access and develop our other forms of intelligence. It isn't our fault; we were conditioned that way. Until as recently as the 1980s, emotions were dismissed by many as insignificant – merely a nuisance or noise – and best ignored. Recent scientific developments challenge conventional thinking on the intelligence of our bodies including how emotions are made, what the primary role of emotion is and, most importantly for the workplace, how emotions influence our performance and profitability.

I invite you to begin a journey with me and I want you to go beyond. By reading this book you will be seeing the world through my lens, my interpretations, perspective and experiences. You bring your own set of experiences and meanings with you, your own lens. This lens enables you to go beyond what you read here to refute what I've written or reconsider things you might have previously taken for granted, a re-cognition.

Whilst I draw on the remarkable work of others, I ask you to keep an open mind as you read. I believe that knowing more about yourself, how your brain and body works, is empowering and enables you to understand more about your own resources and resourcefulness. I've included a selection of concepts and theories that resonate with me. I've interpreted concepts in my own way and by drawing on some of my experiences. I've also included some insights and stories shared by *Life Beyond the Numbers* podcast guests. If any of them resonate with you I encourage you to go deeper. We live in an age where there is so much accessible to us that it can be daunting to know where to begin. **Follow your interests.**

Perhaps one key to an open mind is in understanding how the brain works. This involves an understanding of how other parts of our body work too. For the brain does not work in isolation. It is a part of your body, as much as your heart, gut, limbs and nose are. Yet we often speak of these parts in a disconnected way. They are siloed. And if you've ever worked in an organization that was siloed you know how utterly chaotic that can be and detrimental to communication, progress and results.

My journey

I grew up on a small peninsula in Ireland, the most westerly point in Europe. Surrounded by sea, I grew up in a sea of homogeneity. Almost everyone was white, Catholic and a large part of the population lived off the sea and the land. It seemed like everyone was related and if not, they knew who you were. My dad was what was known as 'a blow in' as he moved to the town my mum grew up in. I attribute a lot of my exploration of life to that single non-conformity aspect of my childhood. Dad had lived and worked on board merchant navy ships and seen so much of the world. His eyes were open to more than what was in front of us. He instilled in us a sense of curiosity, exploration and most importantly humour.

I can also attribute my success to some forward-thinking teachers. Those who saw beyond the traditional career paths of teaching and nursing for girls and encouraged us to broaden our horizons. Funnily enough I aspired to be a teacher, a physical education teacher or a sports coach. Reflecting now, I believe it was less about sport and more about my captivation with what we could do when someone sees us for who we are, our potential and the ability we have to surprise ourselves when encouraged, supported and challenged.

My upbringing was privileged, I believe. That doesn't mean life was always easy. Society has a way of chipping away at your psyche. Regardless of how the familial unit were and school was, there were extended families, community and religion to contend with. **We are the sum of our experiences.**

Our path in life comes down to the choices we make. To make well-informed or optimal choices we can access more than our cognitive intelligence. You might favour brain over body. I'm advocating for you to consider both.

I pursued a career in accountancy. It intrigued me. I was mesmerized by how everything always balanced. It was just a matter of figuring out where both sides of a transaction belonged. It was a bit like breathing – numbers in and numbers out. Figuring out how transactions worked in relation to others was always like a puzzle or play. And I could sit for hours happily unravelling previous years errors in order to present a proper picture of the present to prepare predictions for the future. Of course, that present was always in the past by the time the numbers were presented. And I think that might have been one issue I had with accounting. I spent a lot of time using past information to predict the future.

A job I was both terrified of and exhilarated by got the better of me. Or maybe I got the better of it by realizing there was more to life than numbers. Numbers provide information that needs to be in context to be correctly interpreted. Unfortunately, they can be misinterpreted or manipulated. Over the years I debated with people about what they were saying, I was asked if they were wrong or if they could tell a different story. To make the numbers lie, people must lie first. But when everything is in the right place, free from errors, they offer an irrefutable version of a story.

Balancing a set of financial statements is a thing of beauty. It is ok if you laugh at that. But honestly believe me when I tell you that there is beauty in the act of balancing a set of financial statements. It is futile to compare that to the beauty of a loved one, a sunset or a sunrise. Despite accounting being formulaic there is scope for mistakes and errors. A single mistake or error can undermine integrity. And if unnoticed it can breed and unravel later.

Somewhere in my career a personality test suggested I had a rare trait – being as good with people as I am with details. This reawakened something in me and I redirected my attention to people. I deepened my own understanding of myself and others and began to see the unique beauty in all of us. No single formula will ever generate the same result. **We are, each of us, unique.**

The divided self

This book isn't about fitting in or standing out, but more about the beauty of discovering what is possible when you learn more about your brain and body, including emotions. I do think there is more to life than numbers, metrics or the quantifiable and think some of our thinking needs a rethink, or ways of doing things need a refresh. We deal with uncertainty all the time but by trying to force certainty we miss out on some of the qualitative aspects that might emerge.

This book isn't about getting rid of numbers, metrics or the quantifiable. They absolutely have value. It is what we do with the data that counts. **It doesn't have to be an either/or it is more about 'both/and'.**

Work is where many of us spend a large part of our lives. We may even forge our identities there. Some of us thrive and others barely survive. But the vast majority of us are forced to play by rules that do not always encourage us to be our best selves but rather a version of ourselves, also known as 'professional'.

In the Apple TV series *Severance* people have some sort of device implanted in them so that their professional self and private self never meet – they switch back and forth entering and leaving the office. Their 2 worlds are neatly divided but it takes a toll. In *Cassandra Speaks* author Elizabeth Lesser writes:

> 'The separation of "private speaking" from "public speaking" is a man-made construct. It stripped the emotional from the rational, the heart from the head.

It elevated individuality over connectivity instead of honoring both.'[1]

When I joined the workforce, I was under the mistaken illusion that who I was at work and who I was outside of work were separate. There was no room for emotions or listening to my gut or heart. Yet I brought all of me to work every day. No wonder the battle between reason and emotion has raged for so long. It is inside every one of us and made our workplaces worse, not better, as we prioritized rational over emotional.

As a paid-up member of the accountancy profession, I believe it is ok for me to poke a little fun at the heart of the matter. Those of whom you might perceive as the grey, faceless, dull, boring and analytical minded population of the world. Hey, many of us are proud of this reputation. We wear our qualifications like a shield and take our responsibilities and ethical duties seriously. Accounting is no laughing matter. There is no humour in the numbers. How can there be? They are numbers, inanimate, intangible. They serve a function. They are rigid, formulaic and the antithesis of creativity. While there may be a selective demand for creative accountants they are by and large frowned upon. **But none of us are what we do.**

Accountancy is what I did for many years. It is not me, who I am as a person. Our identity is much more than our job title. I hated being in a box, in a corner, defined by my profession, 'just the numbers person' or the 'finance person'. I am a human with fears, dreams, desires, wants and needs that some people couldn't or wouldn't see. There was always a tension between Susan the person and Susan the accountant.

Perhaps if I'd felt free to integrate the 2 more, I'd still be working in the domain of accounting and finance. Perhaps not.

Yet as my career moved beyond the numbers, I couldn't let them go. So, I asked myself what does accounting want from me. Maybe it wants me to question its fit for purpose in the world we live in today. Can it evolve? Without evolution in science and medicine, for example, would we be here today? Accountancy has evolved to deal with some of the complexities of the world, and some of the corporate scandals. Is it time for further evolution?

Intangible yet invaluable

Business has been transformed by the rise of the digital economy which has accelerated the growth of the intangible, or invisible, economy. Tangible, or physical, assets are no longer the major drivers of value in business but our ability to innovate and create intangible assets like online platforms is. For example, a company like Microsoft can easily scale their business by increasing their Cloud server capacity. Their tangible servers are stored in data hubs but the ability to scale and reach more people by hosting intangible Cloud servers increases their value.

An intangible asset is defined as 'an identifiable, non-monetary asset without physical substance'.[2] There is no requirement to value or disclose intangible assets on financial statements and to date there is no agreed approach for calculating their value. Therefore, the value we see on financial statements may not be the actual value of the company as intangible assets can account for a significant portion of its value. 'If you can measure it, you can manage it' is a phrase familiar to many of us. And by default, we likely believe the opposite to be true: if it can't be measured, it can't be managed. **If it can't be measured, can we afford to ignore it?**

The tangible-intangible dilemma has been a subject of debate for decades. The intangible value of companies has grown exponentially in the last half century. Branding, advertising, knowledge-work, algorithms, reputation, customer relationships, data, software and human capital can all be classed as intangible assets and are largely responsible for driving growth. How might we better understand the drivers of value and reframe our thinking and tools?

For far longer than the tangibles-intangibles dilemma we've been embroiled in a rational-emotional dilemma. We have been led to believe that we have more control over our thoughts than our emotions. Our cognitive skills, our rational and logical thinking processes, can be measured with standardized intelligence tests (IQ). Emotions are not as easy to measure. In line with 'if you can measure it, you can manage it' the only option seemed to be to bring our thinking self to work and leave our emotional self at home. How might we balance emotion and professionalism?

The separation of brain and body, reason and emotion has become the widely held traditional view of how we, as humans, function. However, the rational-emotional dilemma has come under considerable scrutiny in recent decades and advances in the sciences are fundamentally changing our understanding of the mind–body connection, how the brain works and the role of emotions. We need to understand how our cognition-tangible and emotions-intangible work together. By challenging our traditional views of how we should be at work, the full value of our emotions could become clearer, which could lead to better decisions, interpersonal interactions and life overall. The challenge is the continued use of a rational lens to account for people's value.

What lies ahead...

Accounting tells a story. Storytelling moves people. So, this book is about telling a different version of a story that might begin to rebalance an imbalance. It is about leading beyond the numbers and still knowing our worth, contribution and value. It is about recognizing people as people and not as numbers on a payroll or statistics in a report. We talk about people being the greatest assets in a business and yet we account for them as an expense. **Is it because we account for people as costs that we don't always recognize how invaluable they are?**

There is a growing concern that organizations are unhealthy and unhappy places to be. In Part 1, we explore some of the reasons engagement levels are so low and put forward a case to account for emotions at work – this involves some *creative* accounting.

Part 2, is an exploration of what makes us human and some more recent scientific discoveries that shed light on parts of our brains and bodies. We look at how these might that have an impact at work.

Part 3, is an exploration of what it means to be human, and this is illustrated with some personal stories. We further expand the *creative* accounting approach.

How might we improve workplaces of the future is what we explore in Part 4.

Please note that for the purposes of simplicity I have used feelings and emotions interchangeably and brain and mind interchangeably throughout the book.

In keeping with *accounting* speak I begin each chapter with 'a snapshot' and end it with 'the bottom line'.

The bottom line is, there is no requirement to read this book from end to end. You can dip in and out, take what you like and leave the rest.

Part 1

Why account for emotions?

1

A growing (or going) concern

'Out beyond ideas of wrongdoing and rightdoing, there is a field. I'll meet you there.'

Rumi

A snapshot: I place a spotlight on the current state of workplaces and the growing cost of leaving feelings and emotions out of them.

Landmines

Have you ever walked through a minefield? Not a metaphorical one but an actual minefield. I have, twice. The first time was in Cambodia in 2007 and the second time in Kurdistan, Northern Iraq, in 2010. I was working as a director of finance with an international organization that cleared remnants of conflict, like landmines and unexploded ordinance.

When I joined the Nobel Peace Prize winning organization, the Mines Advisory Group (MAG), I knew that to get the best understanding I could of the work we were doing I needed to walk in the shoes of the deminers. Prior to 2007, I had been living in East Africa for 4 years and so I was no stranger to crises and conflict. I spent 2 years in Uganda where many people lived under the constant threat of the Lord's Resistance Army. During a 3-month stint in Khartoum, Sudan, I spent a week in lockdown when riots broke out following the death of John Garang, one of the leaders of South Sudan. And in 2005, I spent time in Sri Lanka following the tsunami as well as in Pakistan following the earthquake.

Walking through a minefield was different though. When I say minefield, I mean a part of a minefield, a cleared path. Deminers use equipment, and in some cases animals, to meticulously clear contaminated land, bit by bit, and reclaim it for use. Once safe, the boundaries of the cleared path are visibly demarcated from the contaminated land by signs and tape.

In Cambodia we got to the minefield early that morning. The team leader, Nick, an ex-British Army soldier, gave us a detailed safety briefing. He had my full attention. My focus was firmly on that briefing and I was careful not to miss a word. He clearly laid out what would happen next. We would get to the minefield where the cleared path would be easily identifiable. We would be required to wear personal protective equipment (PPE) to protect our vital organs. Most importantly we were to follow him. He was our guide, our leader. We were to do exactly as he said.

Standing on the edge of that path, in PPE, felt surreal. Adrenalin surged through my veins. Although I knew the land had been cleared it didn't stop an inner voice asking, 'what if… they missed a spot?' **My heart was pounding so loudly in my chest that even as I type this, I can picture the scene clearly and feel my heart rate increase.**

I dug deep. All I needed to muster, to follow the leader to the other side, was trust. I had to trust that my colleagues had done their jobs, and the land was safe. Safe for the community and safe for me.

When I connected with that feeling of trust, I felt safer. I believed it was safe to follow in the leader's footsteps. All I had to do was put one foot in front of the other. Nick guided us safely to the other side. Once I got there, feelings of relief and euphoria coursed through my veins. I never felt so grateful to have a career in accountancy. The safety of the office and the strength in the numbers was beckoning.

For many of us the workplace can be a metaphorical minefield. To some extent workplaces can be a lot more challenging to navigate. When we join an organization, we probably have some sort of onboarding or induction – a safety briefing of sorts. Boundaries are often invisible, no demarcation between where it is safe to venture and what might be considered contaminated or toxic. And when we unknowingly or unwillingly venture across those boundaries we aren't aware of the potential pitfalls. At times it can be explosive.

We adopt all sorts of strategies to keep us safe and avoid danger, over time these can become a burden for us to carry. Being unable to speak up, always watching our backs, justifying or defending our moves can weigh heavily on us. Some of us cling to our technical qualifications or our area of expertise like PPE in order to keep us safe(r).

'Front Toward Enemy'

On the Claymore Mine the words 'Front Toward Enemy' are visible on the device so that it could be placed strategically to ensure maximum damage when denotated remotely. The risk of death, life-threatening injuries, maiming and serious bodily harm was real. That is the reality of a battle, conflict or war. In many parts of the globe remnants of conflict remain a reality for people today. Land is unsafe to use. Unexploded ordinance lies in waiting, hiding in the long grass or just below the surface. Anyone who ventures across its path is a potential target; it is indiscriminate.

Around the world people face their colleagues on a daily basis. Whilst the workplace is not a war zone or the office a place where we are at risk of death or physical harm, there is a chance that you see some of your colleagues as the enemy. Or as you navigate your days it can seem as if you are going into battle, so you choose your battles wisely, hoping to win the war. This all takes its toll and some of us are in danger of becoming remnants of conflict. **Although we are not in physical danger, are we physiologically and psychologically safe?**

There are those of us who feel safe in the workplace environment, in our teams, encouraging us to do our best work. As a result, we collaborate, we create, innovate, enjoy and treat one another with dignity and respect. We feel a sense of belonging as our values align with the values of the organization. We feel a sense of connection with our colleagues as we work towards a common purpose. We trust our colleagues; our leaders and they trust us. We feel engaged and empowered.

If you are nodding in recognition while reading along to that you are in the unique position of being in a minority of people who feel like this. **According to Gallup, approximately only 1 in every 5 people feel engaged at work.**[1]

Engagement is a feeling that you have towards your work that, in a nutshell, enables you face your work and perform at your best. In an organization the level of employee engagement matters in determining financial success and overall performance. **If only 1 in 5 feels engaged, then 4 in every 5 people feel disengaged.**

If you feel disengaged, you show up and essentially put in the hours. You might just be bored as you are underutilized. Some people battle through resulting in burnout, are bullied and lose confidence, self-esteem or self-worth. Others feel they are undervalued, that nobody listens to them or sees them. Some feel unsafe and avoid anything they consider could become contentious.

In turn their workplace behaviours can become the landmines others have to avoid – abusive, argumentative, authoritarian, defensive, demotivated, disgruntled, unethical, underperforming and unhappy – all lurking beneath the surface and all can be explosive.

Are they better off retreating to the trenches so they can avoid the conflict and win the war? Can we put the blame on people who feel disengaged for being disengaged? Especially if in the right environment the conditions would support them to thrive?

A growing concern

According to Gallup, the estimated cost, globally, of this low level of employee engagement is almost $9 trillion.[2] For me, personally, the magnitude of this number is too large to be meaningful. So, to put it in some perspective let's compare it. If you divide $9 trillion evenly among the 8 billion people on the planet, each person will receive $1,125. The World Trade and Tourism Council reported that in 2019 global travel and tourism generated approximately $9 trillion.[3]

Engagement levels in Europe are estimated to be 13% – close to a mere 1 in 10 people. The UK currently ranks 33 out of 38 European countries with an abysmal 9% of employees engaged. A 2023 report from Business in the Community suggests that investing in helping employees thrive could contribute up to £370 billion or 17% of gross domestic product (GDP) to the UK economy.[4] **Can you imagine the tangible – as well as intangible – benefits for people if they felt engaged at work?**

The results of a 2022 McKinsey Health Institute survey indicated that 9 in 10 organizations are offering some form of wellbeing initiative to employees. However, the report suggests that these interventions are predominantly focused on individuals and on treating symptoms but not on tackling the root causes. Toxic, or negative, workplace behaviours account for over 60% of the factors that contribute to or undermine efforts to improve the situation. The authors ask leaders to consider whether they are solving the right problem when addressing employee burnout?[5]

The cost of conflict in UK workplaces is estimated at almost £30 billion annually and is experienced by more than 1 in 3 people, according to a policy brief by ReWage: *The Cost of Conflict at Work and its Impact on Productivity*. Conflict can be constructive. But destructive conflict disrupts workplaces, people's lives and has all sorts of ripple effects. Formal and informal resolution efforts can prove costly. Not everyone reports conflict, and some will simply resign because of it. This means that the full impact might not always be quantifiable or measurable. The authors suggest that the negative connotations surrounding conflict, as well as the lack of a full picture, make it difficult to persuade leaders and policymakers to tackle this damaging aspect of organizational life.[6]

Can we afford to ignore it?

Bored? My apologies. Numbers and statistics have a way of doing that. They can be unfathomable, unrelatable and ultimately off-putting. Numbers, remember, are just a form of storytelling. Once we understand the story, we can take action. In *Making Numbers Count* authors Chip Heath and Karla Starr say that the secret to telling the story lies in leaving numbers out of the story. **'Our brains,' they write, 'were designed to juggle 1, 2, 3, 4 and 5. After that, it's just "lots".'**[7]

Relating to 'big' numbers is difficult – I tend to tune out. Whether the government is in debt by £35 billion or the lottery is £74 million – these numbers are hard to grasp. They are just numbers. They don't feel real. We need to make them relatable, more tangible.

Leading Beyond the Numbers is placing the focus on people, people like you and me. The bottom line is that going to work is a risky business for many people. We can show up, go through the motions and earn a living. Is that enough for you? Is that how you want to spend your days? **Is that how you would like to look back on your life's work or work-life?**

In a conversation with leadership coach Glin Bayley,[8] she sums this up nicely.

> 'How many people trade 5 days of unhappiness every single week for 2 days of freedom at the end of it? What kind of return on investment is that? Who makes that deal? Why would you do that?'

She says it isn't an investment someone would sign off on. Yet there are so many people in jobs that make them sick, unhappy or they behave in ways that are out of alignment with who they are at their core because they've lost sight of that. It might mean people earn less money in the short term, it might not. But she says to ask ourselves:

> 'Is my life just worth that level of misery for 2 days of freedom? Or actually, would I be better off having 5 days of happiness and working in an environment that actually allowed me to experience more of who I am at my core?'

Going concern

At the end of each financial year auditors perform a 'going concern' test as part of the annual audit of an organization. This is to test that the business will continue to operate for the foreseeable future. If this is in doubt the auditors will make a disclosure in the financial statements to indicate that going concern is an issue. At least they should.

You might be familiar with the collapse of UK construction company Carillion, with annual revenues of £4 billion, and of Patisserie Valerie, a popular UK cafe chain, in 2018. **Why did these businesses fail?**

Previous year annual audits had shown a clean bill of health – they passed their going concern tests. However, subsequent investigations uncovered a different account. A Financial Conduct Authority report stated that:

'Carillion recklessly published announcements on 7 December 2016, 1 March 2017 and 3 May 2017 that were misleading and did not accurately or fully disclose the true financial performance of Carillion.'[9]

The Serious Fraud Office charged 4 suspects,

'... with conspiring to inflate the cash in Patisserie Holdings' balance sheets and annual reports from 2015 to 2018, including by providing false documentation to the company's auditors.'[10]

What kind of organizational culture was there at Carillion and Patisserie Valerie? And what of the culture of the audit firms who issued a clean bill of health? The Financial Reporting Council subsequently investigated the audit firms involved and found breaches in their work.[11]

To prepare for a *going concern* test senior management will prepare future forecasts which will be supported by underlying assumptions. How much does organizational culture and individual emotions influence reason here?

Depending on the culture of the senior management team, or on key individual's actions and beliefs, the assumptions might be closer to a work of fiction than the truth. If some rule by fear, does it make others conform rather than raise ethical concerns? Or does ambition blind accountability?

During the audit the auditors will combine the information presented to them by senior management along with the results of the audit work to form their opinion. Can personal relationships between client and auditor influence an objective opinion? Can emotions compromise ethics? **There are 2 sides to the *going concern* story.**

Auditors	Senior management
Year-end audit work	Forecasts and assumptions
Objective opinions	**Subjective** opinions
Audit history and relationships	Culture and relationships

Regardless of how rational and objective we believe we are we are all influenced by our feelings and emotions. Accountability is tangible, ethics intangible. Can we afford to ignore them?

Perhaps the true financial state of these organizations represented a real account of the organizational health. In this book, the financial state of an organization will serve as a proxy for the cumulative emotional states of people who work there. If we don't know the true story beyond the numbers then the numbers might very well be meaningless. If the culture is unhealthy or toxic, covering it up or ignoring it does not make it invisible even if hidden in the long grass or lurking beneath the surface of the numbers. Do you want to work somewhere where you put your own health and well-being at risk on the front line?

Undoubtedly, those with the most influence over workplace engagement levels are managers and leaders. However, all of us can increase our understanding of the benefits and drivers of high(er) engagement. Feeling engaged at work is something that all of us can strive towards and contribute to. As you read this you might think that this is just wishful thinking or some pie in the sky idealistic management speak or fad. Practically speaking there are small steps each of us can take to increase our own feelings of engagement and empowerment. We will explore some in this book.

Now that we have bid farewell to numbers, mostly, it is time to move beyond battles and war metaphors too. Comparing workplaces to battlegrounds is a metaphor that undermines the reality of the context. **Workplaces are collaborative, war zones are combative.**

The rules of engagement are completely different. However, before we dispense with the analogy completely there is one more battle that we need to attend to.

The battle between reason and emotion

Money matters, that is a fact. Organizations need to generate cash to stay in business. Understanding the *numbers* is key. **But numbers don't make decisions; people do.**[12]

The more we understand about how to draw the best from people, the more willing we will be to create cultures that value interpersonal collaboration. Collaboration relies on connection, and genuine connection requires us to communicate with one another effectively, even when it feels uncomfortable. A business is made up of people, and the better people are treated, the better they will perform. The better people perform the healthier the financial results will be.

Money matters to people too. When co-facilitating leadership development sessions with the effervescent Helen Joy, we are always surprised by how many people in management positions mention money as their primary motivator. When we dig a little deeper, we uncover other motivations. **Asking a simple question like what gets you out of bed every morning is usually a great start to this discussion.**

There are numerous theories about motivation to explore. I like the 3 elements of purpose, autonomy and mastery that Daniel H. Pink writes about in *Drive*. On YouTube you can watch a wonderful animation of these 3 elements illustrating that money is less of a motivator with tasks that require more than basic skills.[13] **Money does matter to people. But it isn't the only thing that matters or motivates.**

- **Do you know** what gets you out of bed each morning?
- **Do you know** what matters most to you?
- **Do you know** what motivates the people you work with?

Relationships are built by being able to connect with people, understand their unique perspective or their view of the world. Getting to know our colleagues reminds us that we are working with people. People like us. Real people with real lives and real feelings. Trust is a foundation, a building block – without trust people won't thrive. Trust requires vulnerability, respect and courage. Courage to put one foot in front of the other and lead people safely. Courage to show up to work daily and do your best. Courage to meet people where they are at and to communicate in a way that they understand. **Courage to take responsibility and say I don't know, no, or not now.**

Healthy working relationships equip us to walk along cleared paths… and not only survive but thrive.

Leaving emotions out of the workplace equation has resulted in an epidemic of conflict, disengagement and mistrust. The traditional approach of favouring our rational side and allowing it to be prominent, dominant, is outdated and counterproductive. But bringing emotions in requires more than *just* talk. Feelings, like numbers, are a form of information. It is how we interpret them and work with them that counts.

The bottom line is: We are all emotional beings, and it's time to invest in accounting for emotions at work rather than counting the mounting costs of ignoring them.

2

Back to basics

'A life spent making mistakes is not only more honourable, but more useful than a life spent doing nothing.'

George Bernard Shaw

A snapshot: In this chapter, I touch on the critical elements of all businesses – people and money – and adapt the balance sheet to tell your personal story. Money doesn't make decisions, people do.

To owe and to believe

Luca Pacioli, an Italian monk and mathematician who lived during the Renaissance, is widely recognized as the father of accounting. Jane Gleeson-White, in her book *Double Entry*, writes that Pacioli defined the double-entry bookkeeping system as 'nothing else than the expression in writing of the arrangement of [a merchant's] affairs'. The purpose of every merchant, he said, is 'to make a lawful and reasonable profit so as to keep up his business' and by following Pacioli's system the merchant would always know all about his business and whether it was going well or not. Debits and credits were separated into 2 columns.

According to Pacioli the most important thing to note in Venetian bookkeeping is that:

> 'All the creditors must appear in the ledger at the right-hand side and all the debtors at the left. All entries made in a ledger have to be double entries – that is, if you make one creditor, you must make someone debtor.'

These terms, debit and credit, both come from Latin and mean to owe and to believe. They are the foundations, the basics, of accounting.[1]

Undoubtedly the world of business and commerce has evolved since the Renaissance period. The basics of how we account, however, are still underpinned by Pacioli's work. **To whom do we owe the credit to for 'a lawful and reasonable profit' becoming profit maximization?**

In 1970, economist Milton Friedman published an essay in *The New York Times Magazine* entitled 'The Social Responsibility of Business is to Increase its Profits'.[2] It does make for a compelling read and broadly speaking outlines a case to separate personal (social) from professional (corporate) responsibilities.

Is it time for a revision of this division? His words cemented a focus on profit maximization. They influenced the role of business in society, a culture of short-termism, perhaps even a culture of profit at any cost. Many people in businesses around the world believe that this version of *business as usual* is not in the best interests of people and planet. **What do you believe?**

Storytelling

Accounting is a simple, yet elegant, way of conveying the story of the financial state of a business and its financial performance. To the external world this story is told through the medium of the annual financial statements. These statements are a high-level summary of every financial transaction that took place during a specific period – typically a year. So, financial statements tell the story of the year gone by through the language of accountancy. Your degree of fluency in that language helps you interpret the story. But the story is *a snapshot* at a point in time and while it might be possible to read between the lines you are seeing the end result of the year in comparison to the previous year.

Each financial transaction tells a story. There are 2 sides to every story and a financial transaction is no different. A financial transaction is an exchange, a movement in and out – much like your breath moves in and out. Every financial transaction has an impact on the balance sheet. The transactions interact with one another, are interconnected and represent relationships with borrowers, lenders and owners.

The movement or the change between this year and last is where the story is – this is the story that matters. The story is in the daily changes in earnings and expenditures between what the business owns, is owed and owes. The story is in the decisions that are made that influence all of the cash movements in and out.

The basics

Cash is the lifeblood of a business. Managing cash movements, in and out, is a critical aspect of managing a business. A business can survive without making profit, but it cannot survive without enough incoming cash to cover the cash going out. Ideally you have cash, like savings, for anything unexpected that might arise. Without adequate cash to cover debts arising a business can go bankrupt, bust. Focusing on profitability without a focus on cash can result in the loss of the business and it is a reason why businesses fail.

There is something else that a business needs to survive, and thrive, besides cash. People. To start any business, you need 2 things – cash and people. The people bring the plans, the projections and predictions, the vision. Cash is a tool to bring those to life. Of course, we hear all the time that people are a business's greatest asset. In what sense? Not in a financial sense, as an asset is something that the business owns or owns the right to use. And while it might seem like your life is owned by your employer at times, your life is very much your own.

Financial statements

Financial statements consist of 3 reports used to tell the story of the business – the profit and loss account, the cash flow statement and the balance sheet.

Profit and loss account

The profit and loss account summarizes how profits, or indeed losses, were generated. A profit is generated when earnings exceed expenditure, and a loss is generated when expenditure exceeds earnings. Note the use of *and* in the profit and loss account. This, to me, is a clear indication of and expectation of both profit and losses rather than a profit or a loss. It is even possible for a loss-making business to have a healthier cash-flow position than a profit-making one.

A profit and loss account can also be called the statement of financial position or an income statement. I wonder if the latter unfairly shifts the emphasis to income or earnings only. Earnings are obviously a key component of a business, but it is unrealistic to think that a business can function without expenditure.

Cash flow statement

The cash flow statement shows the change in cash position between the previous and present accounting period. This statement was developed to provide more details on where cash flows internally and externally. I love that the word flow is attached to cash in this way. Cash*flow*. Cash needs to flow. Cash is the lifeblood of the business. Cash is not profit. Profit is not cash. More profit does not indicate more cash as we can earn cash before we receive it and there is a risk that those who owe us never pay. And a loss doesn't mean there's no cash. But the bottom line here is zero cash equals zero business.

Balance sheet

The balance sheet is always in balance. The balance sheet doesn't demonstrate how profits and losses were generated or where cash was spent and earned, but the cash balance is visible. It does demonstrate a snapshot of the business's financial health at a specific date in time. It is the key to unlocking how financially stable or resilient a business is.

The balance sheet uses a simple equation:

$$\text{assets} = \text{liabilities} + \text{equity}$$

- **Assets** include what you own or own the right to: cash, equipment, a brand, inventory, goods and services paid for in advance and cash owed by customers who bought on credit.
- **Liabilities** are debts you owe to suppliers, lenders and even to customers who paid in advance and whose order is yet to be fulfilled.
- **Equity** is how much the business is worth to the owners, on paper at least – the value of what they have invested, plus profits, less losses and less any dividends paid out to them. The business might sell for a different value but if this number is increasing or decreasing year on year it can provide a view on the financial health of the business. If this number is negative, a business is technically insolvent.

What story does the balance sheet tell?

The balance sheets of businesses vary year on year and between businesses. Every balance sheet will always be in balance but not every business is balanced in the same way and the story that the snapshot tells varies too. To demonstrate this, I've created some charts, with publicly available data, for a selection of different businesses from a variety of industries over a 5-year period. The charts are accompanied by a brief comment.

The equation: assets = liabilities + equity ·

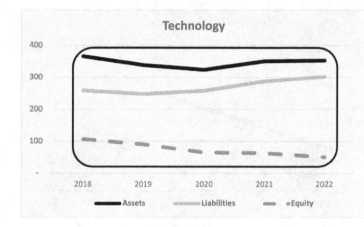

Chart 1 Technology

In Chart 1, we can see equity has been decreasing while liabilities have been increasing. Although not visible this business is profitable and holds a healthy cash balance.

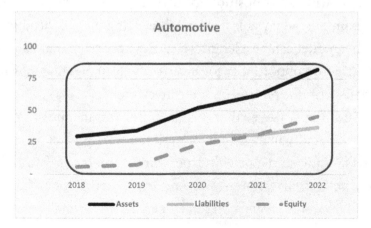

Chart 2 Automotive

In Chart 2, equity has been increasing and liabilities have been relatively stable. This is a relatively young business and has become more profitable in recent years. It has a strong cash balance.

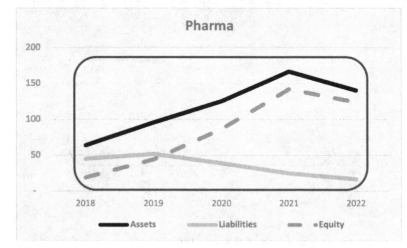

Chart 3 Pharma

The business represented in Chart 3 makes losses on an annual basis, yet equity grows. Some pharmaceuticals operate with a loss position for several years before products are commercially viable or profitable. Bringing new products to the market can be a lengthy and risky process. That can be an attractive opportunity for investors who are willing to wait longer-term for returns on their investments.

In Chart 4, we see that this disruptor was in a position of negative equity in 2018 and its liabilities were greater than its assets. Many start-ups will experience a similar situation as they need to invest in growth and expansion prior to being profitable. This business has been generating annual losses.

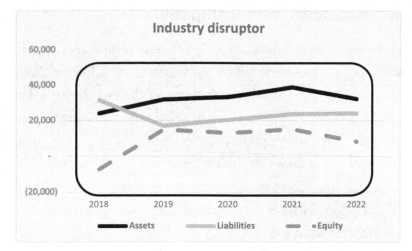

Chart 4 Industry disruptor

The global business represented in Chart 5 has a strong portfolio of brands with a focus on innovation. It is a relatively stable business with a reasonably consistent annual financial performance.

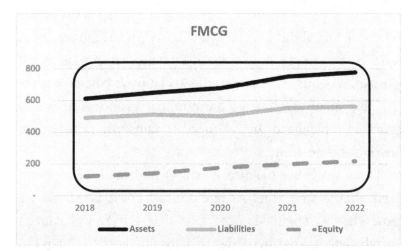

Chart 5 FMCG

Incomparable and incompatible?

Each business is unique. So, 5 different businesses with 5 different balance sheets telling 5 different stories. Even if their balance sheets appeared more comparable the story beyond the numbers would differ. These charts provide 5 annual snapshots. We can make assumptions, draw inferences or arrive at a conclusion. But do we ever really know what is going on?

Much like each person is unique. Your life can be told in numbers too. Each year on your birthday your age increases by one number from the previous year. Does the number on your birthday tell your story? Or is the story in the details, the months, weeks, hours, minutes and moments between last year and this year? What are your earnings and expenditures? What represents your lifeblood? How do you maintain balance? What are your assets, liabilities and equity? Are you surviving or thriving?

What is balance?

When we talk about balance what do we mean? Do we mean equal? For example, both sides of a balance sheet must equal – the total debits and total credits will always equal. Balance can also mean a sense of harmony or proportion like to maintain a balanced diet we need to consume nutrients in the right proportion.

Does work-life balance exist? Is it something that we need, should strive for? As one podcast guest asked, 'do we grow when we are in balance?'. Do we need to be unbalanced or imbalanced to grow? Does that sound wise? Let's explore these questions of balance further with an experiment.

A personal balance sheet

Have you ever thought about using a balance sheet to account for your life? In the following experiment I've adapted the accounting equation (assets = liabilities + equity) to represent a lifetime. I am attempting to give a balanced view of how humans can account for their lives and work out a balance that works best for them.

We are always in balance. Always. Although our debits will equal our credits there may not be harmony and proportion within them, but they are balanced, nonetheless. The proportions can and will vary throughout our lives.

What would make up our assets?

Assets consist of body, brain, breath, senses and systems – your resources. Your body is yours for your lifetime and your external appearance and internal aliveness are uniquely yours. The basic operating systems of humans is the same but not one other person has your fingerprint, your left leg or your exact experiences.

What is our lifeblood or cash equivalent? Energy. Our energy is our fuel. Our energy is constantly in motion as that sense of aliveness we have. Energy enables us to focus, think, decide, learn, walk, run, work, laugh or cry. We can spend more energy than we save, save more energy than we spend and maintain balance. Many of us feel we are lacking in it and we need to work at maintaining it.

What would we include in our liabilities?

In our uncertain lives there are 2 absolute certainties. The first is that you were born. And the second is that you will die. Our mortality is not in question – we are all destined to die. That is a certainty, a fact, a truth. We don't know when or how but we know that one day we will. For the purposes of this simple equation, *we owe death our life*. And therefore, death is a liability. There will be other liabilities through our lifetime, like taxes that will be mentioned later.

How would we calculate our equity?

This one is unique to you. It will include your cumulative profits and losses – mental, physical and emotional. And it also includes what I am simply going to call your essence, what makes you, you and uniquely you at that. For example, your identity, values, potential, strengths and other things that matter to you. These might vary and be stronger at different times during your lifetime.

My personal balance sheet

For illustrative purposes my basic balance sheet equation is made up as follows: assets = liabilities + equity

My **assets** are represented by my brain, body and sense of aliveness, my energy*flows* and I am a continual work-in-progress.

My **liability** is to death + my **equity** represents a life well-lived, in my opinion, that isn't undermined by regrets and what ifs.

My lifetime is represented by 4 separate snapshots in Chart 6, and below – at birth, age 25, age 50 and on my death.

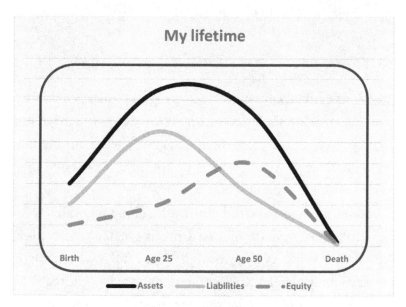

Chart 6 My lifetime

Birth

Assets: On the day we are born, we are fully alive, we are breathing in and out and our systems are ready for action. We are baby versions of who we are today, and we begin to shape ourselves to the world we inhabit as well as being shaped by it. We are totally dependent on at least one other human being to provide our shelter, nutrition and care.

Liabilities: All things being equal death is a long way off. We owe our life to death, we won't outlive it, but we might live long enough to be at peace with it or even to welcome it.

Equity: We don't necessarily have a sense of self, our identity isn't formed, we aren't as yet rooted by our values. We bring some aspects of ourselves to help safeguard our survival, including some biases. We want to survive. A supportive, safe and loving environment will help us to thrive.

25 Years

Assets: We are always a work in progress, always learning, growing and developing. Our brains change throughout our lifetime. We are alive, there is energy flowing through us every single day. Some parts of us are more developed than others, stronger than others.

Liabilities: Death is, hopefully, still a long way off.

Equity: We have developed a much greater sense of self. We have our values even if we might not be fully aware of them. We have multiple identities and one or some might really be at the forefront of how we see ourselves, the world and our place in it. Much of this might not be totally conscious.

50 years

Assets: I turn 50 in 2023. I believe my body is still strong, fit and healthy. And my brain is in good working order. There are parts that might not perform as they used to, but I don't believe the best is behind me. Menopause took its toll over the last decade but thanks to a medical intervention I feel like myself again. I see myself as a work in progress and still see potential, room for growth and development. I am full of life.

Liabilities: Death is getting closer. I've escaped it thus far. I don't know when it is coming for me, but chances are at this point in my life (and certainly how I'm depicting it in this book) there are fewer days ahead than behind.

Equity: I've got more clarity on my sense of self, my self-value and the value that I bring to the world, what matters most to me, what my purpose is and my vision. I've enhanced my self-awareness. I've accumulated a series of profits and losses over the years and have built some reserves. I've also paid myself some dividends. I have an understanding of what, for me, a life well-lived looks like.

Death

Assets: This is purely hypothetical and for illustration purposes only. I will take my last breath though. The act of simply writing that I will take my last breath takes my breath away. But it is a certainty. I will no longer be a person, my body will remain, as with that last breath my aliveness will cease. There may be some residual value and perhaps part(s) of me can be donated to science.

Liabilities: There will no longer be a liability owed.

Equity: As I draw that last breath my hope is that there won't be any last remaining things to tick off a list, things I really wish I'd focused on or experiences I'm still yearning for.

I know I've been loved, and I know what that feels like. I know I've loved, and still do, and know what that feels like. There may be some people who will mourn my passing, miss my presence and keep me alive in theirs. I hope I'll have fed my curiosity, lived by my values, believe I did my best to be true to myself and feel calm and composed. Sounds like a life well-lived to me.

Did you ever think that when you started reading this that the financial statements could evoke emotion in you? Ha! I did.

This is about us as people, as human beings and our inherent or intrinsic value. This is not in any way, shape or form related to monetary values or financial worth.

If I hadn't provided an account of my life in words, would you have grasped what was going on from the chart?

The balance sheet is balanced, both sides are equal to one another. We know this because we used the accounting equation (assets = liabilities + equity). But what about the detail beyond what we see – how do we know if the balance is proportionate for optimal health and wellbeing?

How well do we look after our assets, liabilities and equity? Is it proactive, reactive, luck or a combination? Are there differences in the way we manage our mental, physical and emotional wellbeing?

This *creative accounting* approach allows 3 parts to the equation. So, while both sides of the equation are in balance there are numerous ways to make that happen. This leaves you to think about what your preferred balance might be, allows for flexibility and adaptability and serves as an indicator of when you might need to rebalance an imbalance. We will explore this in greater detail in Chapter 7.

Accounting is a logical, formulaic methodology that tells a version of the story of the financial health and performance of a business. I said earlier that there was beauty in balancing a set of financial statements. The intricacies that underpin the workings are wonderous. But the real beauty is in people and in seeing people be their best selves. The intricacies that underpin our workings are wondrous too, and not one particular combination, input or formula will ever generate the same result.

The bottom line: It is more than debits equalling credits – it is about understanding the balance and harmony within and between them.

Part 2

Human beings

3

Accounting for the brain at work

'The happiness of your life depends upon the quality of your thoughts.'

Marcus Aurelius

A snapshot: An overview of neuroplasticity and the main role of our brain in our life.

In the dark

'Nothing good ever came out of the dark', the priest said. We were a group of 17-year-old girls, and he was a local priest who regularly visited our class. There was something *off* about him. You could sense it, feel it and yet he was a priest. He had the power, the authority and was somehow above reproach. I remember recounting what he had said to my parents, in his sex-before-marriage talk, and my dad said to me 'next time he says that ask him where he was conceived'.

None of us like being kept in the dark. At work this is something that many of us grapple with. When we think we aren't fully informed or that the directors aren't being fully transparent, or our boss is keeping things from us, we assume we are being kept in the dark. Nothing good ever came out of the dark.

And yet there is a part of us that we value so highly that is always in the dark. Our brains. Our brains are in the dark, permanently. Inside our skulls lies an organ that is completely in the dark. Close your eyes for a moment. Darkness. This is what it is like for your brain. It relies on your senses to help make sense of the world. Our brain needs our body to interact with and relate to the world.

Technological advances are constantly shining a new light on old means. Computers, for example, were only introduced in my school in my final year. When I joined Deloitte in 1996, I could only access the internet in the office if my laptop was physically wired to a connection. When I went to work in Uganda in 2003, to send management accounts to Dublin I transferred them onto a USB stick and walked to the nearest internet cafe to access a speedier internet connection. Fast forward to a 2023 podcast conversation in which a guest told me that in their shared services department they have 2 robots working between midnight and 6am that do the work of between 22 and 48 people depending on the day.

Technological advancements have opened up new frontiers in understanding how the human brain works and taken us beyond many of the popular assertions and beliefs that prevailed. Technologies, like functional magnetic resource imaging (fMRI), have enabled neuroscientists to conduct research on how brains function while watching the brain in action.

Old dogs, new tricks

Some beliefs that were widely accepted when I was growing up included:

- Our brains don't change much after childhood, except for brain cells dying off.
- Our brain sleeps when we do.

In her captivating book, *Seven and a Half Lessons About the Brain*, distinguished neuroscientist and psychologist Lisa Feldman Barrett demystifies common misconceptions about the brain, including the view that emotions are automatic responses hard-wired from birth.

- Our brains change throughout our lives. Everything we do changes our brain. My brain is changing as I write, and your brain is changing as you read.
- When we sleep our brain is still active. When we are resting and not particularly thinking of anything our brain is active.

Neuroplasticity is the term for the brain's ability to learn and adapt throughout our lifetime. Neuroplasticity is happening for all of us all the time. It is how our brain operates. The widely cited Hebb's Law is more commonly stated as *neurons that fire together, wire together*. In other words, if the same neurons fire together over and over the wiring strengthens. Repetition strengthens neural connections and the intensity of the firing, or the more multi-sensory neural connections involved the stronger the connections. The neural pathways you use more frequently are more active and ready to fire. **'And social interaction'** according to neuro-scientist Stephanie Cacioppo 'is often the very thing that drives these vital changes inside the brain'.[1]

I was in the car recently, and a song came on the radio that I had no idea when I heard it last – decades ago maybe. It was *Hunting High and Low* by A-ha. The words just seemed to come out of my mouth, from nowhere, as I sang along. I can only guess that I sang that song when I heard it on the radio, when I watched the video and when I danced to it. That is neuroplasticity in action – those neurons that fired strengthened every time I sang that song.

Neuroscientists are discovering more about neuroplasticity all the time. Brain researcher Dr Lara Boyd explains ways in which neuroplasticity changes our brains in support of our learning in the aptly named TEDx Talk: *After watching this, your brain will not be the same.*[2] She says the biggest driver of change in our brain is our behaviour and our brain is shaped by everything we do as well as what we don't do.

She says the research demonstrates that the more challenging something is the more learning that is involved which makes structural changes to our brain. You may have heard about the London taxi drivers who had structurally larger parts of their brain because of all the routes they memorized.[3]

The most effective way to learn anything is by repetition. So, if you want to learn something new, for example, it stands to reason that the more you practice the more you will excel. Dr Boyd explains that while it is the most effective strategy it isn't always that straightforward. **There is variability between our neuroplasticity patterns indicating that not**

everyone is capable of learning in the same way or learning the same things.

For example, you might master accounting without any major effort but struggle to learn architecture. There is no right or one way to learn. Our neuroplasticity is unique to us. **Accept your uniqueness. Let go of comparability and embrace variability.**

Comparing your ability to learn or applying someone else's approaches to learning might be more of a hindrance than you realize. **Variability means their brains are different and so what and how they learn will be different to you – not better, not worse, different.**

Neurons that fire together wire together and the more the same pathway is used the more active it becomes. This can have advantages and disadvantages.

It is advantageous for learning. But if you learnt something a really long time ago and the neurons haven't fired for a while it can fade. I speak Irish (Gaelic). I did all of my schooling through Irish, except English. I was fluent then. I'm not now. Although I have no doubt that if I began to speak it again, listened to it on the radio, read through Irish it would start coming back to me and I would strengthen those pathways that were formed in my childhood.

In school I found accountancy easy, it was fun. My ease at learning it probably convinced my teacher that is what I should do after school. Me as well. There is a big difference, however, between finding something easy to learn and pursuing a career in it. **How many of us pursue careers because we found something easy to do in school and that ability was encouraged?**

Doing what you are good at

Jo Hunter, founder of *64 Million Artists*, spent a large part of her life being a self-proclaimed 'massive perfectionist'. In a podcast conversation she told me that up to the age of about 8 she loved to play, create shows and dances. At times she felt she was a bit too much for people, but she knew people enjoyed her joy and energy and so she tried to balance it out. At school she was clever and was encouraged to do what she was good at.

> 'I think the more you're encouraged to do the things you're good at, as we are in school, we start to focus on those things and not necessarily the things that we love, or we enjoy doing for fun. What I think I stopped doing was just having a go or experimenting or trying. It all became about being the best at something or being good at something or being perfect at something.'

Jo was doing really well and was living a life in which she was really successful. Now she wonders how long she may have continued like that. A life event, a big breakup, was a catalyst for change.

> 'I was in quite a big job and suddenly everything became a bit too much and I became really overwhelmed and stressed. I started to have panic attacks. When I started to deal with that, I realised how much background anxiety I had just been carrying around through the pursuit of perfection. All the time, every day, trying to keep all of the balls in the air so that no one would know how much effort I was having to go to do everything.

It was so exhausting and draining. I didn't even know that that is what I was doing.'[4]

Jo explained that this built up slowly over time, that she was raising the standards for herself daily and creating false expectations from others. She was, she said, responsible for her own unhappiness but couldn't even see it.

Our expertise results from practice, strengthening connections and pathways. The more we do something, the more familiar, natural or *right* it can seem.

Does our expertise preclude us from considering other perspectives? Are we open to learning about other ways of doing things?

Changing behaviours can be challenging – as the neural pathways are fully formed and familiar, easy to fire. They are habitual. In the words of Aristotle, 'We are what we repeatedly do. Excellence, therefore, is not an act, but a habit'. Some of these pathways can lead to us becoming addicted to certain things, including how we think. We can become stuck in repeated behaviours and fail to see another perspective.

This is the way we do things around here

If neuroplasticity is how we do everything, there are implications in our workplaces. It is fantastic for routine predictable work. But so much of what we encounter is uncertain. It is important to remember that when it comes to making changes individual preferences and patterns need to be a consideration. People prefer their way of doing things because that is how they know how to do it, that is the pattern that is wired and fires effortlessly.

Making changes means learning something new and the ability to do that can vary from person to person. We talk about people being resistant to change. People do need to want to make a change and even then, learning new ways of doing things is costly for our brains and it takes time for new pathways to wire. Knowing it is possible for us to change is empowering but change isn't always easy.

If you think about when you join a new organization, you wonder if you will ever get to grips with their jargon, acronyms, policies and ways of working. It can be exhausting in the beginning and the learning curve can be steep. But with a desire to change, focus, attention and practice you get there and wake up one day fully immersed in the culture. It is as if it happens by osmosis. If your line manager and colleagues support you, you might get there quicker.

We wire our brains to our environment and our brains get wired by the environment we are in. This contributes to keeping a workplace culture alive. We might say we are institutionalized if we stay in an organization beyond a certain length of time. But to be part of the culture, part of the environment, to belong, we need to wire our brains to the culture of the organization we join, the culture of the team we join, the acronyms, the politics, the unwritten rules and more.

Think again

We have a high regard for our cognitive abilities. Our ability to think is a valuable part of our identity. You might, like me, pride yourself in your ability to think rationally and objectively. So, it might surprise you, like it did me, that our brain wasn't designed solely to think. **In fact, according to Lisa Feldman Barrett our brain's most important job is to keep us alive, ideally thriving and not just surviving.**

It needs to be able to run all the systems of our body as efficiently as possible by deploying the right resources to fulfil our upcoming needs, even before they arise. Our brain isn't trying to scrimp and save, rather it is concerned with deploying resources wisely and maintaining balance. To do that it needs to be able to predict the resources we need like a form of budgeting. In the next chapter, we will dive into what Lisa Feldman Barrett calls 'body-budgeting' in more detail.

In *How Emotions are Made* Lisa Feldman Barrett explains how our brain predicts everything. It doesn't react. If our brain reacted to every situation, we might walk into traffic or off a cliff. Predicting does a more efficient job of keeping us alive. Our brain forms a prediction, a best guess, based on the situation we are in and creates a plan for action.

Each moment we are awake our brain receives approximately 11 million pieces of data. The majority of this data is visual. We are only aware of about 40.[5] The data, which our brain filters, comes through what we see, hear, touch, taste and smell and also from sensations like our heart beating, our stomach rumbling, aches and pains.

Our brain combines the external and internal data with our past experiences (memories) as well as the situation we are in to make a prediction about what to do next. Lisa Feldman Barrett explains it like this:

'Your brain asks yourself in every moment, figuratively speaking, *The last time I encountered a*

*similar situation, when my body was in a similar state,
what did I do next? The answer need not be a perfect
match for your situation, just something close enough
to give your brain an appropriate plan of action that
helps you survive and even thrive.*[6]

Your brain is predicting, or making meaning, of the
world from the perspective of your experiences, your sense of
hearing, sight, smell, taste, touch and your inner sensations.
It draws on your past experiences to make sense of what this
data means relative to what is happening in the present so it
can figure out what you need to do.

Predict and protect

When we are born our needs are basic. We need sleep,
hydration and nutrition to survive; touch, connection and
love to thrive. We begin to learn about the world through our
interactions in the world.

For example, if you put your finger on a hot stove and you
got a shock, cried or screamed the sensation of being burnt
was scorched into your mind. You might even bear a physical
scar as a reminder. Once the tears stopped a responsible adult
probably told you that the stove is 'hot' or 'dangerous' and
to 'stay away'. This was an expensive lesson to learn; being
burnt was costly in terms of redeploying certain metabolic
resources away from their normal activities so they could
respond to the situation that wasn't predicted. But once
burnt, twice shy.

A beautiful partnership – brain and body living and working together in harmony. A memory is formed in our brain of our experience with the stove. The sensation felt in our finger is communicated to the brain to accompany this memory. And if we heard the words 'hot', 'dangerous' and 'stay away' we will associate them with the experience. So, the next time we are toddling about and come across a stove that looks novel and shiny and is calling out for us to play with it our brain predicts what will happen if we touch it and saves us from another unnecessary expense.

Now imagine for a moment that you've never seen a stove. And someone tells you to stay away from it because it is hot and dangerous. Would you? Would you take their word for it? Or would you be a little bit curious about this shiny new object? Could it really be harmful? If you didn't trust the person warning you, would you heed their warning? Or would you have to find out for yourself? Maybe you'd plan to sneak back later when they've left? One way or another you will make your mind up. To believe or not to believe. To touch or not to touch.

This is where knowledge and experience differ. I can intellectually grasp that this stove, according to that person, is hot and dangerous and I should stay away from it. My brain absolutely gets this. It isn't rocket-science after all.

But just because I *get it* doesn't necessarily mean I believe it. I haven't experienced it. It is a story that my brain has bought into – my brain has heard about things that are hot and dangerous and best avoided. And because my brain is concerned with keeping me safe it takes notice of that story.

If I trust this person, I'll probably believe them. If I don't, I may well have a burning desire to experience it for myself.

The experience is what counts. The experience must be meaningful to you or to me. To make it meaningful we will need to value it or be reminded of how costly the encounter was. Humans make meaning and have been called *meaning making machines*.

As I type in this document my brain is predicting what I am going to type next. And as you read your brain is predicting what the next word you read will   .

Believe it or not that is what it is doing. Did you notice the 'be' appeared in believe and that 'be' is missing from the end of the previous paragraph? We can be surprised when our prediction is incorrect or isn't what we expect.

Imagine you order a coffee *to go* in your local cafe. You leave and as you walk down the street and take the first sip you realize it isn't coffee. This is a surprise. It wasn't what you ordered. It wasn't what you expected. If it is meaningful to you, it will be added to your repertoire of experiences and every other time you drink a coffee someone else prepares you might briefly wonder, before the first sip, could it be something other than coffee? If your brain dismisses it as not relevant, then you are unlikely to think about it again. **What makes an experience meaningful is that it is meaningful to you.**

And this is something you feel. For example, you might have felt anger towards the cafe and decide never to return. Next time someone suggests meeting there you tell them you don't like that place, even if you can't remember why. But there are some internal signals going to your brain that help make that decision, that choice. Your brain takes that past experience + the state your body is in + current situation and makes what seems to you a perfectly plausible and rational choice.

These inner signals are data, information and it is up to you how to interpret them. They aren't always accurate or true. So, for example if you decided that every single cafe was cheating you and you won't ever go to one again you might find that you've curtailed your life for something that in all likelihood isn't true. But your experiences are your experiences, and you decide what is meaningful for you.

You might have laughed off the whole experience and perhaps believed that you mistakenly took someone else's order and actually that other person has yours. Your brain could downgrade the experience, write it off and not associate any meaning to it so it is unlikely to feature the next time you decide to drink coffee, go to a cafe or that particular cafe.

These predictions are complex. It seems like they happen, automatically. They are largely driven by variations of a basic question that our brain asks: Is this safe or unsafe? Do I approach or avoid? Do I consider this person friendly or hostile? Will this person help me or hinder me?

What impact does this have in our workplaces?

Can you think of a time where you reacted to a situation and thought to yourself *woah, that makes no sense*? At some level it did make sense, to your brain. But just because it made sense to your brain doesn't mean it was right or appropriate to the context you were in. And what about other people?

Do you sometimes wonder why people react the way they do or appear to over-react to a simple instruction, request or activity?

Our lives are predicated by prediction. We may get stuck with some predictions that no longer serve us. In Chapter 6 I share a story that will illustrate this in greater detail.

The brilliant thing is we can change. As we saw earlier your brain is constantly changing. As you read these words new neurons are firing. And neurons that fire together, we already know, wire together. Fire the same sequence enough times and it will embed itself, become common knowledge, just like you know that 2 + 2 = 7. SURPRISE!

Lisa Feldman Barrett calls these surprises, or mistakes, prediction errors – which she says is just a fancy way of saying learning. When your prediction is accurate every-thing seems normal. If the prediction is an error your brain adds the error to your repertoire of experiences enabling it to predict better in future. Making mistakes can help us learn. Learning something in different settings or practicing different ways of doing the same thing can also help improve future predictions.

We are unable to change the past, those memories remain. However, the possibility to improve future predic-tions is real. The more experiences we expose ourselves to, the more foods we try, places we visit, skills we acquire, people we meet, the more we learn new and different things, the more experiences our brain has to choose from. The more experiences we can cultivate, the more data our brain will have to use.

How do we make meaning?

Throughout our lives we amass concepts that help us make meaning of the world and predict action.[7] Some of these concepts are universally shared, like 'chair' or 'flower' and others will be more culturally specific. Some can be workplace specific.

Take a moment to imagine something green. What did you imagine? Something out in nature, a favourite item of clothing, a vegetable, a front door, a car or something else? Being Irish I imagine a green field.

Although we might not all imagine the same thing or the same shade of green, especially with 40 shades to choose from, we share the same concept of the colour. We know what green is. We know because as children we were taught about colours – people showed us the colour and named that colour for us. We formed the concept. In the same way we know what cars are, what clothes are, what computers are.

We all have a concept for what customs and traditions are and there will be a vast variety of concepts. For example, where I grew up, we celebrate Lá an Dreoilín or Wren's Day on 26 December. Traditionally people dressed up in outfits made of straw, played traditional music and walked through towns singing '*The wren, the wren, the king of all birds on St. Stephen's Day was caught in the Furs*'. Today only certain parts of Ireland keep the custom alive. If you mention 'Wren's Day' to people I grew up with, they will immediately have the concept. As you are reading this maybe you are forming a concept of it, or of me and the bizarre place I grew up in, and if you look it up later, out of curiosity, then you will form a better concept. Or better still go see it. It is well worth adding to your repertoire of experiences.

Many professions have their own technical language. If you have ever experienced getting a detailed medical diagnosis from a doctor you might have only understood every couple of words. Yet, they are speaking to you as *normal*. The concepts are clear for them. Concepts can vary through workplaces, industries and professions. In accounting there are many concepts that have a shared understanding like 'going concern', 'true and fair view', 'debit' and 'credit'. People created all of these concepts – people assigned meaning to them and that meaning is transmitted through our language.

Your past experience, or the concepts formed in childhood, through your culture and current context help your brain predict. When we travel, read, listen to stories or watch programmes from faraway destinations, we expand our concepts as we encounter foods, wildlife, words or traditions that we never have before. Concepts are like shortcuts, so we don't have to figure out what things are every time we encounter them.

Real or imagined?

We can also imagine an experience and our brain doesn't distinguish between real or imagined so it adds it to our experiences. Have you ever seen an orange riding a bike or a daffodil surfing? I know I haven't, but I can imagine them.

Chartered psychologist and psychotherapist, Lisa LLoyd, told me in our first podcast conversation that she believes our imagination is our most misused resource. This intrigued me so much that I invited her back for a second conversation to go deeper. She explained that we use it all the time to problem solve and how we use it is critical. If we were unable to imagine, we couldn't possibly think about how something could look like or feel differently in the future. However, 'when we're feeling stressed or anxious, it has a really big impact on imagination. It shuts our imagination down and we end up then focusing on the negative stuff'.[8]

Is it right or left or right and left?

Have you been told that you are more left- or right-brained? I have. We have 2 networks:

1. The default mode network (DMN) also referred to as the emphatic network.
2. The task positive network (TPN) also referred to as the analytical network.

The networks suppress each other so when one is activated, the other tends to be deactivated. In an fMRI our DMN is the one that lights up when we are not doing anything else – hence default mode. And when we are being creative or solving technical problems, whole brain activity is visible. The right/left split is now recognized as over simplistic and was a best guess at what the brain was doing prior to technological advances.

Each network performs a different type of reasoning and is supported by a different type of learning. According to the work of Professor Anthony Jack of Case Western Reserve University:

- TPN gives us sense or the ability to be rational. It for sense-making, problem-solving and decision-making.
- DMN gives us sensibility or the ability to be reasonable. It allows us to be open to other people, to new ideas and to emotionally self-regulate.

At a course I attended, somatic leadership coach Amanda Blake, cautioned that we are at risk of over reliance on the TPN and under using the DMN. Some of us will favour one network over the other but over reliance on either can be a hindrance. Ideally, we want to learn to go between both networks and leverage both. This way we can balance different perspectives and won't deem one way of thinking as superior to another. We need both.

She says that if we want to improve our TPN reasoning style, we can do that by taking in information by listening, reading and taking notes. We can only improve our DMN reasoning style experientially, or through gaining relevant experience.[9] This can involve leveraging our embodied felt sense which we will explore in the next chapter.

The bottom line: Our brains predict and protect and are constantly changing throughout our lives.

4

Accounting for the body at work

'There is more wisdom in your body than in your deepest philosophy.'

Nietzsche

A snapshot: I cover some insights on the body, including body-budgeting, embodiment, our nervous system and our heart.

Beyond the brain

'I think therefore I am', said Descartes. He was believed. Not only was he believed but everything else apart from the brain was seen as less than and to be ignored. And those who suspected that our hearts and gut held intelligence or wisdom were dismissed, denounced and denigrated. The rational case to revere the brain reigned supreme. It is still the business case in many of our organizations today.

Could it be irrational?

Our body holds lots of wisdom. We have countless sayings to reflect this:

- Do you know anyone who looks like they've got the *weight of the world on their shoulders*?
- Have you ever needed to *get something off your chest* or *a shoulder to cry on*?
- Maybe you've been lucky enough to *fall head over heels* for someone or you found yourself *in over your head*?
- How many different activities have you *dipped your toe into*?
- Have you ever *been tongue-tied, paid lip service* or *lost your head*?

Our body is key to our performance. Not just our brain. Our body plays a vital role. I suspect that many of us take our body for granted. We may even mistreat it. Some feel shame about their body and wish for a taller or shorter one, one with perfect abs, toned legs, a thinner one or a different shape altogether. Somewhere along the line we lost sight of the wisdom and focused on the aesthetics. We ascribe our success in life to our intellectual endeavours. When it comes to our body we might dress for success or to keep up appearances. We raise up our brains and put our bodies down. Or we ignore them all together other than as a means to transport our brain. **Meanwhile our brain is focused on keeping us alive by paying attention to what is happening in our body. Are we making this harder than it needs to be?**

How much do you know about how your body works? Do you ever think about your heart or your gut and whether or not they hold any intelligence? Do you know what embodiment is or embodied self-awareness?

We learnt in the last chapter that our brain's ultimate role is to keep us alive. To do this it is constantly predicting the resources like oxygen, water and nutrients needed based on information it receives from the rest of our body – e.g., our heart rate, salt levels, glucose levels. You are not the only one that is in the dark about this. So is your brain. It does this from within the confines of your skull, the back-office so to speak.

All of the systems of our body run in the background, and we are largely oblivious to what is going on. In a way it is similar to the back-office at work. When everything is going well, we almost forget the people there exist and begin to think that maybe we treat them too well. But when something goes wrong it, they are the first to get the blame. **Have you ever thought, *my body let me down*?**

We will never tune into everything that is going on inside of ourselves, we couldn't possibly – there is constant movement of data and resources. Our body is designed this way. However, attuning to some inner sensations might enable us to manage our resources more optimally which can help us perform better. If you feel, or hear, hunger pangs, for example, you know what they are telling you.

Body-budgeting

The brain performs, what scientists call, allostasis to help the body to adapt to changes in the environment. Lisa Feldman

Barrett uses the phrase 'body-budgeting' to describe allostasis. Body-budgeting is our brain predicting, or budgeting, our needs as we expend and earn energy. Some things we do are more costly than others. Learning and moving are 2 of our greatest expenses, she says.

Some bodily processes like blood pressure, glucose levels and temperature need to remain relatively constant within a certain range and the brain facilitates this through a process called homeostasis. Homeostasis maintains our core body temperature regardless of how hot or cold we get. However, if we are ill and have a spike in temperature or when we exercise and speed up our 'body-budgeting' system will allocate resources to bring our body back to homeostasis. Body-budgeting helps our body adapt to changes in our body in order to maintain homeostasis.

Have you had budget responsibility at work? If not, you can imagine for a moment that you have. Certain costs are easy to predict – like staff costs, rent, electricity and so on – they remain relatively stable over a period.

- If you are planning on buying some computers or the services of a consultant, you would budget for that in advance, so you don't come up against an unplanned expense at a later date when resources are scarce, and finance say 'no'.
- You also want to ensure you are generating sufficient earnings throughout the period to cover, at a minimum, the resources required to maintain operations.

In the same way you can't expend energy indefinitely if your energy is depleted. If you are going to use resources to exercise you want to know you have the energy to do so, the investment is worth it and there is a return on that investment.

But let's face it, no matter how accurately you try to predict, changes can happen that will have a knock-on impact on your (body-) budget, and you might end up earning less or incurring a greater expense than planned.

Performance paradox

We have developed an ability to override, ignore and misinterpret our bodily needs as predicted by our brain. Our body is begging us to rest but we persist with our relentless pursuit of productivity. We complain that our bodies want rest as we reach for another coffee, or other stimulant, to provide us with a boost. We are rewarded with an immediate boost happily unaware that our brain now needs to redeploy bodily resources to deal with the additional caffeine in our body. Or we simply push through and carry on.

Embodiment coach and chartered psychologist, Kerry Cullen, calls this the performance paradox. It is a term she came up with after working with lots of people in organizations who were very successful, but she could see were still struggling. What she began to notice was that people, herself included, through dedication and doing their best work, can let go of what they know energizes and restores them to get more done. In our conversation, she gives an example of a typical day from waking up early and thinking:

'I'm going to go for my run. And today I'm going to get my lunch, and then I'm going to make sure I get a walk before I come home. But you get up and you think, actually, I've got that report that I need to finish, and I've got those emails.

So, I'll just get a head start on those first, and then… I'll run at lunchtime. So, you start your day, you're in the report. Next thing you know you don't have much time for breakfast. You're having a cup of coffee or you're grabbing something for breakfast.

Now you're in meetings or you're on zoom, or you're into your day. Then it gets to lunchtime. And you haven't managed to get the report finished and you think I'll just keep working through that and get that done.'

You go through the day constantly feeling a bit behind and by bedtime you have not done anything to restore your energy. Kerry says, 'the more we do that, the more disconnected we are from what actually gives us energy'.

Embodied awareness

Embodiment is about bringing awareness to our bodies and how they are feeling. Kerry describes her coaching work as *enlivening awareness about those resources that are in our body.* She says we all have those resources; we all have an innate wisdom in our body. When we get caught in the performance paradox we lose or override some of that connection and miss out on information being communicated by feelings and sensations. [1]

In a conversation with embodiment coach, Ana Bernardes, she explained the concept of embodiment as us being in alignment between what we think, feel and do. She says throughout our lives we have learned to dissociate from inner feelings because we were told not to feel them. We do this for emotions we don't want to feel because we might think of them as negative or inappropriate. She says suppressing emotions like anger and sadness also impacts our ability to fully feel pleasure and joy.[2]

We have access to embodied self-awareness as well as a conceptual self-awareness. Embodied self-awareness is a felt sense – a sense of feeling sensations inside our body and what our body is sensing in the space around us whether we are active or still. These sensations, like feeling hot or cold, for example, are experienced in the present moment. Our conceptual self-awareness enables us to think about the self – our thoughts, feelings, values, purpose, beliefs and actions. We can reflect on our past experiences, feedback we have received and the influence our culture or society has on us. It enables us to account for the hot or cold sensations we are experiencing. It also helps us to think about the future.[3]

What a feeling

For a moment I invite you to play along with me and imagine yourself winning an Olympic medal or an Oscar. I very much doubt I'll be receiving either of those, but I can still, conceptually, create a picture of what that might look like. Go on, indulge me. Take a moment to imagine what that experience would feel like in your body. You might find that if you stand up it is easier to embody the feelings. Can you imagine the different sensations that you might be feeling when people are cheering and clapping on this momentous occasion? Thinking about our future self and feeling into the sensations we imagine our future self might feel can fuel our fire. Combining a conceptual dream or vision with our embodied sense of aliveness, our inner resources and resourcefulness, can be a powerful exercise. How do you think I wrote this book?

Executive presence

Do you know anyone who has been told that they lack executive presence? Executive presence is an intangible term. We know it when we see someone embody it, but we might not be able to tangibly describe it.

In *Leader as Healer*, Nicholas Janni says that presence is 'what it means to show up with as much of oneself as possible'.[4] To embody a sense of presence requires us to be present in our body. We talk with our body as well as with our words – we walk the talk. We embody our words. We can gain the attention of a room with this level of embodiment. Not in an authoritarian way where everyone pays attention out of fear but in a way that they feel part of something, connected to us. We might be described as charismatic or passionate or as having the courage of our conviction.

Executive coach Sue Rosen described executive presence to me as:

'... inspiring the confidence of other people in your capabilities and your potential, even, or maybe especially, when under pressure. It's this ability to stay calm when there's chaos, to bring a level of certainty when we all know that there is no certainty in business or in the world more generally.'

Whether or not you're an executive are you conscious of how you bring your presence to every conversation and interaction whether it is a one-on-one with a direct report or speaking to a room full of shareholders? Sue says that we need to be:

'... willing to stand up and speak up and be seen but doing that in such a way that people perceive it as, or that we are, authentic and genuine because that's how we build trust and the confidence of the other people that we can get stuff done, that we will be able to deliver.'[5]

Under the hood

As you read are you aware of any pain or tension anywhere in your body? Are your shoulders raised or relaxed? Is your jaw relaxed or clenched? Can you feel your clothes on your skin? What about your breathing – is it fast, slow, shallow or deep?

We live in a world that does not encourage a connection to our body or to the innate wisdom of our body. Even if you are disconnected from yours, others will be tuning into what your body is saying and doing. Many of us can be oblivious to the fact that we are saying one thing with our words and another with our body. When you feel someone is being disingenuous or inauthentic it might be because they are disconnected from their body.

For example:

- they are smiling but you can't see it in their eyes;
- they are telling you that everything is under control, but their shoulders are slumped; or
- they are congratulating you on your promotion but there is no enthusiasm or warmth in their demeanour or words.

Our body can say a lot about us, more than we are often aware of, and most especially if we are not attuned to or connected to it. This line from *In an Unspoken Voice*, by Peter A. Levine describes this nicely for me, 'Despite our apparent reliance on elaborate speech, many of our most important exchanges occur simply through the "unspoken voice" of our body's expressions in the dance of life'.[6]

Making sense of it all

Before we go further let's make sense of our different senses that provide our brain with data.

- **Exteroception** relates to our 5 familiar senses: sight, smell, sound, taste and touch.
- **Proprioception** is the ability to sense where your body is in space. Whether you are standing, sitting, moving, lying down or gesturing this information is being communicated to your brain all the time.

- **Interoception** is the ability to feel our inner sensations – like our heart beating. Our interoceptive network operates throughout our body and different receptors send communications to the brain.
- **Neuroception,** a word coined by Stephen W. Porges, Ph.D, is like the intuition of our nervous system as it is going on beneath our conscious awareness. Our nervous system knows what is happening by scanning the environment for cues of safety and danger. We aren't required to think about it, *we just know it.*[7]

The role of our nervous system

Each of us has a nervous system. The autonomic nervous system is the part of the nervous system that is responsible for regulating our heartbeat, digestion and breathing. It interacts with our hormones and immune system.

It consists of 3 parts:

1. Sympathetic nervous system
2. Parasympathetic nervous system

The sympathetic nervous system is also known as 'fight and flight' and the parasympathetic nervous system also known as 'rest and digest'.

When we are in an active state the sympathetic nervous system speeds up our heart rate and expends energy from our reserves. When we move to a more relaxed state the parasympathetic nervous systems slows our heart rate down and helps restore our energy reserves. For example, when we exercise the sympathetic nervous system activates to supply the increased energy requirement. After exercise the parasympathetic activates to help us recover, conserve and replenish energy. Together these 2 systems perform a balancing act to maintain homeostasis.

3. Enteric nervous system

The enteric nervous system controls the gastrointestinal tract.

Our nervous system is constantly in conversation with our environment including the nervous systems of other people. Our nervous systems communicate with one another and can influence one another which, in turn, has body-budgeting implications. **Lisa Feldman Barrett says that the best, and worst, thing for our nervous system is other humans.**

It has a singular focus on survival and is constantly scanning our environment for cues of friend or foe, approach or avoid, danger or safety. It is vigilant and diligent.

Threat detection

Bodyworker, Steve Haines, explained to me that the nervous system is like an inner guard dog or a sort of threat detection system that is constantly checking is this safe or not. If it is not safe, we go into fight or flight or freeze states. We speed up to survive, or we collapse, disconnect, disassociate and feel stuck. Steve told me that in his experience when people understand that these reactions are our own protective reflexes that are happening unconsciously in the background, it 'is absolutely gold dust'. It helps us to understand that when we go into these states it is because of our individual nervous systems' perception of whether we are safe or not.[8]

Kerry Cullen says we might think of cues of danger being major things like natural disasters or conflict but actually our nervous system is focused on what it perceives as risky, or meaningful, for us. Our nervous system is sensitive to both excessive and insufficient stimuli – for example being overwhelmed or underwhelmed at work, conversations moving too quickly or too slowly, too much attention, not enough attention. So, if we're stuck, for example, in the performance paradox, that is a cue of danger for our nervous system.[9]

Our interactions with others, our status, our acceptance by our family, friends, and community is fundamental to our ability to survive and thrive. In a workplace countless events can be perceived as danger signals for our nervous system, like making a mistake, receiving feedback, the tone someone uses when speaking to us, interacting with someone who is more senior, presenting in front of people and preparing for, or being in, a difficult conversation.

Steve Haines says that most of our threat detection systems are similar to a smoke detector and although it should only go off if the house is on fire it tends to go off when toast burns. Our nervous system can be dysregulated. It can be difficult to live with these alarm signals activating in our system all the time. They take up resources, expend energy and reduce our ability to feel safe and to connect with others. Understanding how to regulate our own alarm signals is, 'a really powerful result of learning to feel and being skilful at interpreting things that often feel a bit too quick and a bit too noisy and a bit too fast'.[10]

Connection

Understanding how to regulate our nervous system helps us to think differently about things that seem to cause us to react or trigger us. When we react to situations it is not about who we are but about how we respond. When we are in our protection states we tend to be self-critical and assign blame. When we are in a regulated state we are more self-compassionate and open. Career coach, David Lee, says it enables us to be 'cool, calm, and connected'.[11] No longer in a protective state it is easier for us to collaborate, be curious, make well-informed decisions and learn. We can achieve a state of flow. We can thrive in this state.

We often think that the reactions of others are because of something we might have done to them. We look for an explanation, we make meaning. But knowing that nervous system moves in and out of these states of protection and connection helps us see how other people's reactions and behaviour stem from what is happening in their nervous systems. **The key for us is to tune into what is happening for us by connecting to these inner sensations.**

By fine tuning our attention on our cues and signals and learning to self-regulate when dysregulated we can become more flexible and resilient which in turn helps us better connect with others.

If you would like to know more about your nervous system, I encourage you to explore *Polyvagal Theory*, the work of Stephen Porges.[12] Deb Dana pioneered the research of Stephen Porges for clinical use, also teaches and writes about it so that we might all learn to regulate or 'befriend our nervous system'. Some of the stories told in Chapter 6 will help to illustrate this further.

Every breath you take

Do you ever think about your breath or breathing? Do you notice when it quickens or slows? Breathing is something that we all do all the time, we have to. But we might only be aware of it when it is difficult to breath, or we hold it or think we are about to run out of it. We can feel our breath, smell it sometimes and you can definitely feel someone else's breath on you – especially if it is unwelcome.

We can use our breath intentionally to help us regulate when we feel stressed or in an anxious state – we can breathe through challenges – it can ground us. It is something we can do for ourselves that is accessible all the time. Even at work when things feel a bit much or you feel anger or frustration rising you can self-regulate by consciously connecting to your breathing.

It takes practice to tune into your breath and the power of it. It isn't as simple as just slowing your breathing down when you are breathing fast as this can be a danger signal to your nervous system. But you can try various breathing techniques and learn to pace your breathing differently. Sighing also helps us to regulate. When we hear someone sigh, we probably think they are bored or annoyed. They might well be. They might also be self-regulating. Take a moment and let out an intentional sigh. How did that feel?

When in doubt return to your breath. By tuning in, listening to the sound of your breath, you can still a busy mind and notice the quality of your breath. With a quiet mind, you may just hear what is in your heart.

Listen to your heart

Our heart is closely associated with the feelings and emotions world. We tend to associate it with love, warmth, passion and romance. We might have a heart to heart with someone or offer them a heartfelt apology or thanks. Some of us wear our hearts on our sleeves and others have hearts of stone. We can speak from the heart and have a change of heart. The heart of the matter is that your heart has value in your life beyond being a vessel that pumps blood around your veins. By paying attention to it you can influence your performance.

Your heart is always on – constantly beating. It is active and has intelligence that we can access. This isn't about leading from your heart or only following your heart. This is more about intentionally involving your heart. Your heart communicates more with your brain than your brain with your heart. It communicates via the vagus nerve which is part of the parasympathetic nervous system. Vagus means wanderer and this nerve system wanders from brain to gut transporting information in both directions. Scientists believe that roughly 80% of the information flow goes up from the body to the brain.[13]

HeartMath

Heart rate variability (HRV) is a measure of the amount of time between your heart beats. Higher variability is associated with higher levels of performance. HeartMath Institute has been researching the heart-brain connection, including HRV, for over 3 decades. Their research has demonstrated that different patterns of heart activity are directly related to how we think and feel. When we are stressed, for example, our heart rhythm becomes erratic and this can impair some of our cognitive abilities – like thinking clearly, learning and effective decision-making. If we can get our heart and physiology into a state of coherence, then our brain will follow. **Coherence is how synchronized our brain, heart, and respiratory system are and enables us to perform optimally and have better relationships.**

Gavin Andrews, MD HeartMath UK and Ireland, told me that in this coherent state our autonomic nervous system is in balance and a synchronized pattern can be seen reflected in the heart rhythms with the technology they have developed. He said:

'Now that does some wonderful things. It facilitates homeostasis. So, you're putting your body in a place where it can renew itself, rebalance itself, self-organise, give you all of the renewal and revitalisation that you need to keep you healthy, basically. And there are also benefits cognitively. When you practice coherence, the brain basically follows. The heart is the largest rhythm maker in the body, and you go into this lovely ordered stable, rhythmic pattern. The impact of that on the brain in effect is that the stress centres sort of deactivate and the prefrontal cortex comes back online again.'

Gavin says when we are coherent, we can be more logical, more creative, more empathetic, more of all of those higher cognitive skills that make us human and the best versions of ourselves. When we are coherent, we are calm and composed. **Being calm and composed is different from relaxation. It is a state between activation and relaxation, where you are calm yet alert and focused, composed yet primed for action.**

You can engage, connect, collaborate, perform. When coherence is measured using HRV the difference in coherence and relaxation frequencies is clearly visible. Relaxation is when the parasympathetic is dominant and if you are in a deep state of relaxation, the brain slows down and it's harder to perform. Gavin used the following example to illustrate further:

> 'If you're on a long-haul flight, you wouldn't want the pilot of your jumbo jet to be mega relaxed when they're coming into land. You want them to be present, calm, but alert. You probably want their average heart rate to be a little bit higher than it normally would be because you want them to be able to respond in a moment's notice, should anything dangerous happen. We don't want them to be too activated, too stressed, because that's compromising as well. For performance, too much or too little of anything is not great. What we want is this state that's somewhere in between. And that's what coherence is. It's a very unique, specific state, one that we can intentionally put ourselves into.'

Techniques that HeartMath have developed incorporate breathing, but their main focus is on intentionally connecting to your heart and generating a heartfelt emotional state. Most of their techniques are designed to be done with the eyes open so that they can be done anytime, anywhere. If you would like to experiment with some Gavin kindly recorded 3 coherent breathing techniques especially for listeners of my podcast *Life Beyond the Numbers*. And if you are curious to learn more about the heart–brain connection there are some wonderful resources on their website. [14]

Gut instinct

Has your gut been communicating with you as you read through this chapter? Our gut also communicates with our brain. The gut–brain connection is an area of emerging research and one to watch. I've only included a couple of titbits to *whet your appetite.*

Our gut is our largest sensory organ. The gut–brain partnership begins very early in life as we learn to communicate about our gut – we might feel, and appear, visibly upset when hungry or satisfied when full. Our gut continues to influence and impact our mood and emotions in adulthood. Our gut microbiome plays an important role in keeping us healthy and each of our gut microbiome is unique. Giulia Enders, author of the delightful book, *Gut* says, 'A gut that does not feel good might subtly affect our mood, and a healthy, well-nourished gut can discreetly improve our sense of wellbeing'.[15]

The bottom line: Your body is your asset – don't take it for granted.

5

Reconciling brain, body and behaviour

'When you are offended at any man's fault, turn to yourself and study your own failings. Then you will forget your anger.'

Epictetus

A snapshot: An exploration of how mood and emotions influence your performance.

You too may have grown up with the belief that to be professional means being unemotional or at least keeping your emotions under control. Some of us are better at being cool, calm and collected (or *connected*) and know how to avoid becoming hot-headed. I mean the last thing you want is to be at the mercy of these erratic and impulsive behaviours, right? So just like the performance paradox you learn to over-ride the data and ignore or squish the emotions especially the ones that feel uncomfortable. Or do you?

The traditional view of emotion was that emotions were automatic responses to specific circumstances. Neuroscience research has challenged this belief that emotions are hardwired into our brains and shown that there is no emotional centre to our brains and the same parts of the brain can be in use whether we are being rational or emotional. We feel our emotions, and how we feel, and act is dependent upon our mood.

What are you in the mood for?

Before we go deeper into emotions it is helpful to understand what mood is. The scientific term for mood is *affect*. Lisa Feldman Barrett says that affect is a *basic accounting* for how we are feeling. It is like a base-line body-budgeting measure that accounts for the story of the moment, a snapshot based on our interoceptive sense. And it can affect how we interact with the world.

Can you describe your mood?

Mood is with us from the moment we are born until we die. We are always feeling something. And our body is always sending internal sense data to our brain. You experience this sense data as your mood along a continuum of feeling calm or aroused and pleasant or unpleasant. Mood and emotion are not the same thing. Mood is more basic than emotions. However, your mood will have an influence over your actions, behaviour, emotions and thoughts. You view the world through the lens of the mood you are in.

We will be more reactive, rather than resourced and responsive, when we are in a more aroused or unpleasant mood, and less reactive when we are in a more calm or pleasant mood. Others can influence our moods and we can influence theirs. We can also influence our own, intentionally and unintentionally. All impact our body-budget.

Introducing Sam and Alex

Sam and to Alex are fictional characters I'm using to illustrate some of the stories being accounted for as we move through the rest of the book. By way of background, you can assume that they were both born in the same year and by all outward appearances they lead very similar lives. They both live in similar homes, drive electric cars, go on holidays abroad and work in a similarly demanding roles in the same organization.

Mood swings

Imagine that you arrive at the office early one morning. You are feeling refreshed and energized. You've had your coffee, and you are ready for the day. You greet Alex warmly in reception and Alex reciprocates. You have a calm, pleasant feeling. And as you take the stairs to the fourth floor this monologue begins in your head:

> I'm feeling good today, my energy is high. I wonder if it's because I woke up before the alarm clock got a chance to rudely wake me. I hate that bloody alarm clock! The word alarm is in itself alarming, and it would be so much nicer to be woken up by something less alarming. I wish whoever invented it came up with a better name for it. In a hotel they offer you a wake-up call – that's way better.

The word alarm always reminds me of that night a few years ago when the burglar alarm rang all night in the house down the street. I didn't sleep a wink and the following day I had that interview. It was a disaster, probably one of the worst interviews ever. I was like a zombie and even though I did my best to make a good impression my answers to their questions were incoherent.

I really wish I had gotten that job. Imagine what I'd be doing now. I'd probably be running the place. Instead, I'm here talking about the same old stuff day in, day out. Nobody listens to me. I can't understand it. It is so frustrating. The changes we need to make are as obvious as the nose on my face. What is wrong with these people?

By the time you get to your desk you are no longer feeling pleasant or calm. Sam passes your desk and chants a chirpy good morning, and you nod nonchalantly. You think to yourself that's odd, why do I feel like this?

We've already seen that we make or assign meaning – it is like we reconcile the state we are in with an account that seems to match that state.

Got it, you think, I should never have walked up those stairs, it drained my energy. I should have taken the lift. Too much exertion first thing in the morning just doesn't suit me. I'll take the lift in future.

You might never realize that you thought your way to that account. Your thinking took you from feeling pleasant and calm along a continuum towards the opposite. Your thinking changed your mood. If you stay in this mood, it will influence what you think, feel and do throughout the day. You could have reached a different conclusion. You can also change your account.

To make effective decisions in the workplace, we need to be in a resourceful state. If we are in a state where we feel fear, anxiety, stress, unpleasant or aroused in some way it can cloud our judgement. It can influence how we go through our day.

What has emotion got to do with it?

Lisa Feldman Barrett's theory of constructed emotion is that an emotion is what your brain predicts how you should feel in a specific situation. Whether you feel frustrated, grateful, hesitant or joyful, is a result of your brain's construction of these emotions from previous experiences in similar situations.

Just like the body-budgeting predictions these predictions are constructed from 3 key ingredients:

1. your past experiences;
2. your inner sensations; and
3. the context, or situation, you are in.

Feelings are information, data, that our brain interprets or makes sense out of so it can predict what our body needs for our next action. Sometimes our brain constructs an emotion to explain what we are experiencing.

We all have concepts of what these emotions are. In the same way we learn about the stove being hot (see Chapter 3) we learn what emotions are. For example, as children:

- When we cried, we may have been told not to feel sad.
- When we heard 'happy birthday' being sung we associated happiness with birthdays.
- When we misbehaved at home or in school, we may have witnessed an adult get cross or angry with us and were told 'don't do that, you know it makes them angry'.
- If we struggled to understand something in school, we may have been asked if we were feeling frustrated.

Much like we know what a stove is or what green is, we have concepts to explain what different emotions are.

Excited or nervous?

Imagine you are on your way to a job interview and perhaps you have a jittery feeling in your stomach, and you feel your heart starting to speed up. Your brain needs to make sense of what is going on in your body and to do that it takes the context into account and sifts through your past experiences to make meaning by asking 'what is this most like?' so it can guide your actions. If this is the first time you've ever been to a job interview your brain might associate these feelings with how you were before your exams and conclude that you are feeling apprehensive, nervous or anxious. Or it might associate these feelings with how you were before a competitive event and conclude that you are psyched up, excited or motivated. And depending on the story your brain constructs to interpret these feelings is how you will feel, or be, in the interview – nervous or excited.

The great news is we can assign different meanings. Our emotions are not absolutes, they are negotiable, and we can reframe them. Recognition of the sensations can lead to re-cognition. We can make prediction errors with our emotions too. But by learning how to tune into these sensations we can improve our predictions. We might not be able to measure our emotions to manage them, but we cannot afford to ignore them. Instead, we can learn to understand them. Understanding how to interpret our emotions can be challenging but like all skills the more we practice the easier it can become.

I'm so emotional!

Have you ever said something like:

- 'It was an emotional week.'
- 'I felt very emotional because…'
- 'That movie was so emotional.'
- 'That person is too emotional.'

Which emotions were you referring to when you used the word 'emotional'?

Emotional includes a whole host of different emotions. Just like food is a generic descriptor of different foods. If you say to your friend, I feel like some food, want to grab dinner? There is a good chance they'll ask you what type of food you'd like to eat.

Maybe you felt very emotional because:

- You got an email from your manager you thought was critical of your recent work.
- You felt annoyed that they hadn't come to talk to you about it first.
- You felt disappointed that your work didn't meet their requirements.
- And you felt afraid that it might reflect badly on your performance.

The more you can describe your emotional experiences, the better. You can actually help yourself manage the situation and begin thinking of ways to resolve it, if that is what you need, by naming what you are experiencing, what you are feeling. **We are rarely feeling one thing.**

Understanding what we are feeling, and why we are feeling that way, is helpful. So, next time you hear yourself use the term 'emotional', have a go at identifying the emotions you are experiencing.

Emotional granularity

Lisa Feldman Barrett describes emotional granularity as an ability to construct more precise emotional experiences and says it is fundamental to becoming emotionally intelligent. One of the easiest ways she recommends to do this is to expand your range of emotion words. More words can enable better predictions which is more efficient for body-budgeting purposes. Greater emotional granularity leads to greater health and wellbeing. **Can you discern between feeling aggravated, exasperated or irritated? How about feeling delighted, elated or overjoyed?**

If your default response to 'how do you feel?' is *fine*; stretch yourself. Tune into how you are feeling and find some words to articulate how you are feeling. One simple way to get started is to download the *How we Feel* app. It is described as:

'A free journal for your wellbeing created by scientists, designers, engineers, and psychologists. Over time, you will learn precise words to describe how you feel, spot trends and patterns, and practice simple strategies to regulate your emotions in healthy ways.'[1]

My friend, Mel, who I recommended the app to said:

'I started with just tracking the beginning and end of the day... then I had a melt down over a situation and as I flipped through the words, I discovered I could let the emotion move through me more easily when I had identified it with the precise word. Emotion is technically how a feeling moves through you. It struck me that clarity had cleared the path of least resistance so I could let go of the situation and my reaction to it.

The short, suggested videos are also quite enlightening. I'm now keeping a tab whenever I feel into something else. Identifying it and tracking what is happening and who is with me is giving me less anxiety and more curiosity. And a greater confidence in articulating exactly what I'm feeling. I'm leaving the why out of it, as I am genuinely curious about the sensations rather than the reasons.'

We can also learn emotion words from other languages and cultures. The first time I came across the Japanese word Amae (pronounced *ah-ma-eh*) it was as if I had known the emotion all my life, I just didn't have a word for it. In *The Book of Human Emotions*, Tiffany Watt Smith describes it as the 'sensation of temporary surrender in perfect safety' in the arms of a loved one, for example, who in their embrace melts all your troubles away. She further describes it as 'the glue which allows stable relationships to flourish, an emblem of the deepest trust'. She wonders if the reason that we don't have a word for this combination of vulnerability and belonging is because we find it difficult to accept the support of others and prefer to pretend that we are always self-sufficient.[2]

- How many emotion words do you know?
- How many do you use on a daily basis?
- When someone asks you 'how you feel' how do you respond?

I notice that people, me included, often ask questions like: 'Are you feeling ok?', 'Are you feeling good?', 'Are you scared?', 'Are you happy?', 'Did that annoy you?' and so on – the answer to these questions will be a yes or no. Asking more open-ended questions like 'How do you feel?', 'How did that make you feel?' give people an opportunity to articulate how they really feel.

Fear the feeling and feel it anyway

You've probably heard the phrase 'feel the fear and do it anyway'.[3] At times we know some of our fears are irrational.

That doesn't make them any less real. All of those fears begin as good intentions – to keep us safe, protect us from harm. Fear is a feeling, an emotion that we construct. These feelings are absolutely necessary at times. If there is a legitimate danger, you don't want to have to think about it you want your fight or flight or freeze response to kick in and protect you.

All of the other feelings that we experience in our lifetime are real too. We don't need to fear our feelings. We need to *feel* our feelings. After all your brain and body (yes, yours) are creating those feelings. You are the one experiencing the feeling. Nobody else is making you feel a certain way. But just because your brain interprets the data in a certain way doesn't make it accurate or true. It doesn't make it irrational either. It is real, it is valid, it is your feeling. Tuning into it, being curious about it and allowing it to move through you helps. Investigate and become curious rather than deny or dismiss. Describe it.

It is ok to feel. It is. It doesn't make you illogical, immoral, irrational, less than, soft, weak, too emotional or unreasonable. You have feelings. Moment to moment you feel. It is when you are not feeling anything you should worry. Well actually there won't be a need to worry about it as you'll no longer be here. Feelings are vital signs of life. We don't have to fear our feelings. **Our feelings are messages and blaming the messenger is futile.**

The message will remain the same. Understanding the message or looking at the message from different perspectives can help you reframe the message.

We can misinterpret our feelings. As Lisa Feldman Barrett so eloquently puts it: 'Heart rate changes are inevitable; their

emotional meaning is not'.[4] Our heart rate can change several
times in a day. It can speed up when we exercise, slow down
when we rest, skip a beat when we see someone we love or
someone who scares us. If you feel your heart beating faster
there may be several explanations for that, and you may not
guess right first time. **Human beings feel. All of us feel.
Feeling is normal and healthy.**

It is how we deal with these feelings that can backfire
on us. It is when we ignore our feelings or deny our feelings
that we can begin to lose touch with what these feelings are
attempting to communicate. And ignoring or denying the
feelings of others is disrespectful and harmful. According to
David Whyte: 'Denial is the crossroads between perception
and readiness; to deny denial is to invite powers into our
lives we have not yet readied ourselves to meet'.[5] At times
these coping strategies will protect us. We might not be
ready to accept something and so we can dismiss or deny
what we are feeling until we are ready to accept or at least
be curious.

Becoming more aware of your inner sensations and what
they are trying to tell you requires paying attention to them
and practice. There are many ways of doing this including
mindfulness and meditation. Steve Haines told me that it
takes practice to learn how to feel and to realize that:

'Feelings aren't a beacon of eternal truth. They're
a negotiation. They're always real because they are
a perception side of you, but it doesn't mean that
accurate, useful, or true. They're things that need

to be negotiated, that we can reframe and construct them differently. That might need help and support.'[6]

In his book, *Anxiety is Really Strange,* he says, 'Changing feelings is often counter-intuitive. For many people, strategies are based on trying to relax or ignore difficult feelings as they emerge.'[7] We need to be able to discern what our feelings are attempting to communicate to us. And the only we can do that is by feeling them. Interpreting our data dissolves difficulties.

What makes a conversation difficult?

We put difficult in front of things at times – 'difficult conversations' or 'difficult person' or 'difficult encounter' or 'difficult decision'. What is the opposite – easy, simple, straightforward? What makes these difficult? **Or maybe the better question is what makes them *feel* difficult *for you*?**

A conversation or a person or an encounter or a decision are not in of themselves difficult. They are what they are. What is difficult, for us, is how we feel about them. They stir up something inside that makes it difficult for us as we would probably rather not feel it. To cope with that we might procrastinate, delegate, avoid altogether or go ahead without understanding what they are communicating and make a mess.

Two of us can face the same conversation, the same person, have the same encounter or be presented with the same decision and yet both of us will think, and feel, differently about it. We might have similar experiences, but we won't have identical ones. Our reasoning will vary. Our approach will vary. And what is going on inside of both of us will vary too. Variation is the norm.

We might agree that Alex is a difficult person. But have we actually sat down and talked about what that means? Do we agree on what we believe makes Alex a difficult person? And how does Alex feel about this? Does Alex know that they are considered a difficult person?

Difficult is a catch-all. We immediately know what we are referring to even though our individual understandings or experiences of what feels difficult for us might be very different. And rather than explore why we consider the conversation, person, encounter or decision difficult we justify our reaction.

Don't get me wrong I've encountered my fair share of difficult conversations, decisions, experiences and people.

What is really going on?

In accounting there is a concept 'substance over form'. Which means that rather than simply looking at the form the information takes when presented we need to examine the substance. It is often illustrated with this simple example 'if it looks like a duck and quacks like a duck, it's a duck regardless of whether or not it is presenting as a goose'.

Let's take the 'difficult conversation' and explore the substance over the form of it. The conversation itself is nothing more than a conversation – that is the substance of it. The form is a frame or a description. And what feels difficult for you might feel easy for me or vice versa.

Why do we use the label 'difficult'? Perhaps because we do not feel fully equipped, at some level, to deal with it. Our nervous system is communicating with us. There are inner sensations warning us to avoid the situation. We might not be conscious of them but as we've already seen that doesn't matter, they are happening regardless and if our nervous system is concerned with keeping us safe then that is what it is going to do. It is working with our brain to reconcile an account of the conversation we'd rather not have or the person we'd rather not hang around with or the encounter we wish to avoid or the decision we do not want to have to make.

So, what do you do about that?

I once heard a keynote speaker who had accomplished an incredible feat and was hugely inspiring and their advice was to run through every single scenario beforehand so that you are prepared for every eventuality. And I remember thinking to myself 'how exhausting'. And yet I also see the sense in that because our brains don't know the difference between what we imagine and what we actually do. So, if we rehearse different scenarios then we are creating this repertoire of experiences to choose from and feel more prepared.

Is there another way?

When it comes to us:

- We can tune into our state, the feelings of discomfort or unease, rather than dismissing them.
- We can get curious about the information that is being given to us rather than ignoring it.
- We can work with it to understand when it feels more or less intense.

When it comes to others, we can separate the behaviour from the person and label the behaviour instead of the person. For example, rather than saying:

- Sam is a procrastinator, we can say something like: I notice that, at times, Sam procrastinates.
- Alex is a demanding person, we can say something like: Alex tends to be demanding.
- Alex and Sam are optimistic, we can say something like: Alex and Sam have optimistic attitudes.

You can do the same for yourself. If you are used to telling people that you are an ambitious person, tell them instead that you have ambition. And if you are feeling uncomfortable with whatever is being discussed separate yourself from that too – you feel uncomfortable, you aren't uncomfortable.

There's no business like show-business

Difficult situations in the workplace are not confined to the corporate world.

Remember when Will Smith slapped host Chris Rock live on TV during the 2022 Oscars ceremony? Do you have any idea how you would behave if something similar happened to you? Imagine for a moment that you are Chris Rock. Picture yourself in his shoes as you watch Will Smith walk toward you on stage. How would you have reacted as the events unfolded? Or put yourself in Will Smith's shoes; what would you have done if Chris Rock told a joke at your or your loved one's expense?

The reality is you'll never be certain as to how you would react in their shoes. And try as you might to be prepared for such an event, as Mike Tyson famously said, 'Everyone has a plan until they get punched in the mouth'. But what if you had a tool that could help you better manage your own reaction when things don't go quite as expected?

Try RULER on for size

At the Yale Centre for Emotional Intelligence, Dr. Marc Brackett and his team have developed an evidence-based tool for increasing emotional intelligence they've called 'RULER.'

RULER is an acronym for the 5 key emotional skills involved. Emotional skills can be learnt, practiced and refined. Research shows that enhanced leadership skills, greater workplace performance, conflict-resolution skills, better relationships, less anxiety and greater wellbeing are all associated with them.[8]

1. **R** is for **recognizing** emotions in yourself and others. In others, you'll recognize changes in their face, body or voice. Awareness trumps accuracy here.
2. **U** is for **understanding** the causes and consequences of emotions and how they influence your thoughts and behaviour.
3. **L** is for **labelling** emotions. Emotions are information or data. The more accurately you label them the more nuanced and greater your understanding will be.
4. **E** is for **expressing** your emotions in a way that is appropriate to the situation.
5. **R** is for **regulating** emotions with helpful strategies.

The first 3 skills (RUL) enable you to identify what is happening and the last 2 (ER) empower you to self-regulate emotions. Although you never know for certain what someone else is thinking or feeling you can try situations on for size and empathize.

Put yourself in their shoes

Let's use the RULER tool and apply it to the infamous Oscar's scene. If you need a refresher, rewatch it first.

	Chris Rock	**Will Smith**
R	What do you think he was feeling as Will approached him? Do you think he ever imagined that Will would slap him?	What do you think he was feeling? Do you think it ever occurred to him that Chris' joke wasn't meant to cause offence?
U	Although he seemed to take it on the chin, did he want to strike back? Did he have to restrain himself? Did he understand the consequences if he did? Or is he unflappable?	Did he understand the underlying cause of his outburst? If he had known that he would publicly disgrace himself and be banned from attending the Oscars for 10 years, would he have behaved differently?

L	What word would you use to best describe his emotional state? *Terrified. Confused. Humiliated. Composed.*	What word would you use to best describe his emotional state? *Rage. Furious. Disgusted. Livid.*
E	'Will Smith just smacked the **** out of me'. He seemed to express himself by making light of the situation and laughing it off. Was that appropriate to the context?	He seemed to express himself by stomping, slapping, shouting and swearing. Was that appropriate to the context?
R	Do you think he felt in control? Was he regulating his emotional state? Did you notice him pause? Did that allow him time to compose and calmly deliver 'That was the greatest night in the history of television'.	Did he seem like he was in control? And if he had paused, for a moment, do you think he could have behaved differently?

Don't look back in anger

Chris Rock has insisted he is over the incident and doesn't hold any bad blood towards Smith. It was widely reported later that he said, 'Anyone who says words hurt has never been punched in the face'.

In November that year, Will Smith' appeared on *The Today Show* and told host, Trevor Noah, that there were nuances and complexities to why he reacted that way but at the end of the day, he just lost it. He acknowledged it was not the right way to behave. He said he was going through something and that we never know what is going on with people. When Trevor asked him what he learned? He replied, 'We just gotta be nice to each other man, you know, it's like, it's hard'.[9]

I've used this scenario when co-facilitating leadership development sessions and in a recent session one of the younger people suggested adding another R, for reflection, to the end of RULER. RULER-R. Love that. Reflecting on the situation can help you understand how you dealt with it and how you might have dealt with it differently or will do in future should something similar happen.

Who's naughty or nice?

With so many competing priorities in work and life, it isn't unusual to feel stressed or overwhelmed when things don't go according to plan. No matter how prepared you are a surprise, a change or disruption can impact even the calmest of people. You can lose your temper, say something you regret later or burst into tears.

- When you, or someone you know, reacts in a way that seems inappropriate to you or the situation, dig deeper. Start with recognizing and understanding your own sensations and reactions.
- The next time someone rubs you up the wrong way take a moment and pause. During that moment breathe deeper, get curious and ask yourself 'what would my best-self do in this situation?'

- If you are on the receiving end of an unwanted reaction, ask yourself if something is going on for the other person? If the situation allows you can ask some questions to find out more.

The simple act of interrupting your reactions or behavioural patterns can help you discover and develop new strategies, so you respond differently in the future. Practice the RULER-R technique and refine those key skills. And remember 'we just gotta be nice to each other' even if it is hard.

- **R** Recognize
- **U** Understand
- **L** Label
- **E** Express
- **R** Regulate
- **R** Reflect

What is emotional intelligence, really?

Do we associate the word intelligence so much with cognitive intelligence that almost unknown to ourselves we disregard the bit where we have to experience emotions and feel feelings? Do we instead believe that knowing that emotions and feelings exist is enough?

Of course, we've experienced emotions but there is a time and a place for them, and we know how to keep our own in check, out of the office and under control. If we are being professional, then we can't be emotional. And our emotional intelligence (EI) is there to help us recognize emotion in others. Right?

We never really know what is going on for another. We can make a guess based on what we see in front of us, but we cannot be certain. For example, I've cried when I was happy as well as when I was sad. I might smile even if I don't feel like smiling inside. Emotional intelligence starts with us.

Self-awareness is a first step, a key. It isn't enough in itself, but it is a step in the right direction. If you had asked me in my mid to late 30s if I was self-aware, I would have told you that I was. Now I will tell you that it is a work in progress, and that as I expand my awareness, I realize how much practice it requires. In Chapter 4 we explored the difference between conceptual and embodied self-awareness.

How do you know that you are aware is a question I often ask podcast guests. It seems like a trick question. Being aware of the self, our whole self, includes our thinking self and our feeling self.

- Do you think about your thinking? Do you reflect on how you think?
- Are you aware of different thought patterns that you have?
- Do you believe everything that you think?
- Do you know how to change your thinking?
- Do you know how to slow down your thinking?

Clients often tell me that they can't stop thinking. I was like that too. Until I heard someone say years ago, 'take your thoughts for a walk, don't let them take you.'

Thinking and feeling are 2 different things. When we say 'I think I feel' or 'it feels like' we are thinking, not feeling. **We feel our feelings.**

Tuning into an awareness of how we are feeling and what those feelings are trying to tell us takes practice. I think we can jump to conclusions and settle on the first thing that we think it is about. The practice seems to be in less thinking and more feeling and tuning into letting the feelings speak for themselves. That is what the next chapter is about.

The bottom line: You are not your feelings or your thoughts, you feel your feelings and think your thoughts. Separate the behaviour from the person.

Part 3

Being human

6

I'm only human: not rational or emotional but rational and emotional

'A human being is always full of contradictions.'

Seneca

A snapshot: Personal accounts from me and my podcast guests to illustrate some of what we covered in Part 2.

Pause

This chapter is intended like a pause. It provides an opportunity to reflect, process and digest. As you read through this chapter notice:

- if you recognize any of the concepts that we have covered; or
- any thoughts or feelings you might have. You might want to explore them further.

I was perfectly comfortable reflecting on my experiences and drawing out how I believe they relate to what has been covered so far. You may see them differently. I also selected some stories from podcast guests that, for me, also illustrate some of the concepts. However, these are their experiences and so I am simply paraphrasing their stories without interpretation. You are welcome to do so and keep in mind that it will be your interpretation of their story.

All in my head

I largely ignored the role of emotions or feelings in my life. They were there but I didn't understand the importance of them. They often seemed inconvenient and best ignored. I took my body for granted and didn't know much about the needs of my body other than the basics.

I developed back pain in my mid-20s while backpacking through Asia enroute to Australia. I remember getting a twinge on the lower left-hand side of my back. This was data or information from my body that I wasn't quite sure what to do with. On arrival in Sydney, I got a job. Some days when I got home from the office I would lie on the floor as it was the only way I could get relief from the pain I was experiencing.

On the ground floor of the building where I was living there was an elderly Chinese gentleman who practised acupuncture. I tried acupuncture with him for a couple of weeks. One day he told me that he could continue to treat me, but he knew that he was only providing temporary relief and I really needed to get to the root cause. I went to see a physiotherapist who told me that back pain was inevitable as we were meant to be on all fours. After examining me she told me that there was nothing wrong. But there was.

Over the next 12 to 15 years, I saw people who practiced all sorts of different methodologies – medical professionals, holistic practitioners and a whole host between – in countries around the world. Many provided temporary relief; some helped, and others really didn't. I remember one orthopaedic specialist telling me to buy a book called *Treat Your Own Back* – their way of telling me they couldn't help me any longer. Actually, I think they said that it was all in my head. At that time, I was still under 30 and some evenings I cried with the level of pain I was experiencing. I went for x-rays and an MRI. Nothing showed up.

I could function fine, mostly. I went to work. I went out. I went on holidays. I moved to Africa to live and work. I learned to live with the pain. I accepted it, reluctantly. I was so worried about injuring myself that I made sure that any activities I undertook were low risk. I never lifted anything heavy. I worked on my posture. I experimented with all sorts of core strengthening routines and found ways of coping or working around it, of managing it. I shaped myself to my reality. It became a huge part of my identity. But the pain impacted my life and often flared at inconvenient times. Over time I began to notice that when my life was going well there was little to no pain. And when times were more stressful it was present.

Learning to feel

I still remember my first appointment with Steve Haines. I was in my early 40s and living in Geneva. The first thing he said to me was 'you are too young to live like this'. As I lay on a table in his office, he asked me how I felt. I replied, 'I think I feel …'. He said something like 'I didn't ask you what you thought, I asked you how you felt. **How do you feel?**' I didn't know what he meant by that. And more importantly I didn't know how to describe what I was feeling. I began to tune into what my body was feeling. Then he asked me how my legs felt. 'Useless' I said. I didn't think about that response, it was how I felt. It was also news to me.

For my homework he recommended that each night once I got to bed, to spend a couple of moments feeling my feet. It wasn't about moving them or touching them but about directing my attention to them, of being aware of my feet. That was the beginning of a new journey. After a few nights I began to dream of running. It was like I'd unlocked something and my legs or feet were saying to me remember when we used to run, we'd love to do that again. Within about a year of meeting Steve I ran my first and only, to date, half marathon.

Through working with Steve, we uncovered a likely root cause of this pain that I was feeling. When I was 11, I broke my elbow. Badly. I had to have 2 operations. In the first one they failed to put me back together again. In the second I had 2 pins inserted into my elbow to reattach the bones and more than 20 stitches. I spent about a week in hospital and a further 6 weeks with my elbow in a cast. When the cast came off, I couldn't straighten my arm out – it was locked at the elbow. I went through months of physiotherapy which was extremely painful at times. Even now, almost 40 years later, I feel a shudder go through me just thinking about it. During the recovery period the surgeon told me that if I ever broke my elbow again, I would lose the use of it permanently. That is quite a thing to be told as a child. I took it to heart. That message was meaningful to me. I made sure that I prioritized protecting my elbow.

I embodied that protective mechanism. I began to look through the world with that lens. Steve explained the likelihood of what was going on for me like this: if you have a house alarm, it will usually sound when someone breaks in. However, my alarm was sounding when a leaf fell from the tree in my garden. The pain I was feeling in my back was down to my extra vigilant nervous system. It was seeing danger everywhere and doing its best to keep me protected. This account needed a refresh. The past was not going to change but the future could.

I'm elated to say that pain disappeared. Not overnight. It took time to convince my body and brain that my elbow didn't need extra protection. Even as I improved, I experienced flare ups, particularly when I travelled. As soon as I sat on a long-haul flight, I would feel that pain. I learnt to reassure myself that I was safe. I did this by whispering quietly and compassionately to myself, inside, that I had not injured myself in any way and this pain was unnecessary. I was sending the message that I didn't need to be on high alert – that the data that I was getting from my body was inaccurate. It worked. The pain would fade.

I had my doubts about what I was doing but as it worked for me, I kept going. I still hadn't encountered the work of Lisa Feldman Barrett or heard of Polyvagal Theory. And a few months later I had a further revelation in a session with Steve.

What's CrossFit got to do with it?

As I began to get confidence back in my body, I joined CrossFit Geneva. I was so happy to be doing different types of exercise after years of not doing much more than walking and swimming.

It was a 6.30am class on a Friday morning and we were practicing handstands. I didn't really want to do them. There was a group of us together, the early risers. The thing I love most about CrossFit is if you haven't mastered a movement the coaches will find an alternative that works the same muscles. This particular morning the coach offered to help me with the handstand. I reluctantly agreed. Next thing I know I am doing a handstand, and the coach is holding my ankles. I felt uneasy, a bit anxious. I asked to be let down and much to my surprise, the surprise of my coach and the others in the group, I burst into tears.

What the hell?

I was in the dark. Whatever about not wanting to do a handstand or not enjoying the attempt, I couldn't account for being in tears.

The next morning, I returned to CrossFit determined not to let that experience dissuade me from CrossFit. CrossFit is meaningful to me. And I had never felt uneasy like that in a class before, but I didn't want the association to lock in. Luckily there were no handstands. However, I couldn't get what had happened out of my head. I couldn't understand why it had happened or I couldn't explain my reaction.

During my next visit with Steve, I recounted that incident. And he said to me, 'Without thinking tell me when you last felt like that'. And suddenly I was transported to a scene that had occurred over a decade earlier. I was upside down in a Toyota Hilux pick-up that had overturned twice on the road somewhere between Kampala and Queen Elizabeth Park in Uganda. The data from our senses isn't always accurate. This was another prediction error.

Our experiences matter

This is why many of us will react so differently to the same thing and why doing a handstand put me into a spin while everyone else looked at me strangely. A handstand for them was safe, fun even. It might be a bit weird and challenge their proprioceptive senses but our brains like challenge, novelty and new experiences. Being upside down feels unnatural, proprioceptively, unless of course you've had lots of practice. But instead of embracing the novelty my brain was fixated on what happened the last time I was in this situation when my body was in this state. The state was influenced by the situation and the only account I had was I felt a sense of panic at doing a handstand.

I still go to CrossFit; it has value in my life. It is meaningful to me. I love the variety of movements. I love expanding my comfort zone by being challenged and challenging myself to lift heavier weights or improve a gymnastic routine or simply connecting to my body and feeling the power of my strength. Two classes are rarely the same so I'm also adding to my experiences and increasing my predictive ability. My maximum deadlift, to date, is 88kg (194lbs). I vividly remember when I first lifted 85kg (187lbs). I felt so exhilarated as I smashed my previous personal best. I walked home from CrossFit that day smiling widely and feeling 6 foot tall. Sometimes when I need a boost, I remind myself of that experience and it helps me find courage or inner strength. It reminds me that I am capable and that I can do things I never thought I could. I still have absolutely no desire to do a handstand but **now it is a choice more than a fear**.

CrossFit is an expensive hobby for my brain to deal with. Lots of resources are deployed to get me through a class and because no 2 classes are ever the same my brain is stumbling around when it comes to predictions. At times an inner voice complains incessantly hoping I'll ease up or stop. But I reap the rewards of my efforts. Even writing about this has paid an energy dividend. I corrected my posture and I'm smiling as I type and feeling strong. CrossFit is an investment that keeps paying dividends and I don't even have to be in a class for that to happen, I just have to think about it. As I do, I'm reminded of the sign that hung over the entrance in Geneva: *it never gets easier, you get stronger*.

You're fired

During my career I became really good at firing people. I put this down to the first time I ever had to do it. I was working in Uganda, and we uncovered some theft at the office, investigated it and found conclusive evidence. Unfortunately, someone had to lose their job. I was (feeling) seriously uncomfortable with the thought of firing this person. My boss told me that he would be more worried about me if I didn't feel something – and reminded me that I was human.

Instead of focusing on the inner sensations warning me to fight or flee I decided to put my focus on the human who was about to lose their job. I got through the 'difficult' conversation. It was difficult. The conversation itself wasn't difficult but the way I felt and watching how the other person reacted was difficult. It wasn't something I particularly wanted to do again.

It is a crap experience to have to fire anyone but by doing it in a way that makes the experience as pleasant as I possibly could for the other person changed the way I approached them. Every time I had these conversations, I got better at them. There was still data warning me to avoid the conversation, but I expected that and put it down to being part of the preparation. As long as I kept my focus on the other person, I got through it.

The last time I had to let someone go the circumstances were slightly different. They hadn't passed their probation. But still, they were senior and so it came as a shock. I wasn't their line manager – the line manager was unavailable and there was a timing issue – so I volunteered. I didn't volunteer because I became so good at difficult conversations that I now enjoyed having them. I volunteered because I knew that I could do it with compassion.

In the intervening 15 years I lost count of the number of similar conversations and disciplinaries I was part of. I can honestly say it never got easier. But I got better at it. Every single time, without fail, I would feel my body prepare for what was ahead. My bowels would always empty, sometimes several times before the conversation. My system would be that bit quicker and singularly focused. Now I understand that this was preparation for a fight or flight response that I needed. What I was going through was natural, par for the course.

Sounds of silence

Over the years I also collected my own data about how people reacted or responded. The thing that stood out the most for me was that when someone got a shock, they often went quiet. I think we get so used to speaking when someone else stops it can be hard to interrupt that pattern. But what I learned to do was to remain silent. That took practice. But what people seemed to need was time to compose themselves. It is difficult though to sit still, remain silent and watch another human suffer.

As the shock began to sink in for the person, I was usually asked to repeat what I had said. And oftentimes people asked this several times. I found that short statements worked best. Sticking to the point and stating the facts. The facts didn't always give a lot of satisfaction, but the reality was that the person had lost their job, and it was my role to help them understand that. These conversations lasted anything from 20 minutes to a couple of hours.

I did need to pay attention to what was happening in my body and to my body language. Pretending to be compassionate isn't the same as acting from a place of compassion. I was in the room for the other person, not for myself. I now know that our nervous systems were in conversation with one another. I always felt uncomfortable but could discern those feelings from feeling unsafe.

The conversations became contentious at times. One disciplinary hearing stands out above all the others. This person ran rings around me. Everything I presented; they had an excuse, defence or story. It was like a game of cat and mouse from the get-go and at times the cat showed their claws. Remaining composed was taxing on my body-budget. I felt under immense pressure. Parts of me were screaming to go into the other person's story and *prove them wrong*. But a part of me, the part that helped me perform under pressure and remain composed, prevailed. The person didn't lose their job, that day.

Some of the disciplinary or termination conversations did not go well. I could have handled them better. **Being able to reflect and take personal responsibility for how you show up and how you behave is what counts.**

I think the difficulty with these conversations is that we believe that our emotions might get the better of us and that our reactions are automatic, that we cannot do anything about them. That isn't true. By paying attention to what is going on inside of us, we can access our own resourcefulness and resilience. It doesn't mean that this is easy, but we can get better.

I remember with the very last person, the one who didn't pass their probation, after the news sank in and the documentation was signed, I had to go back to their desk with them while they cleared it and gathered their belongings. This was difficult. The person was crying. I was torn as part of me felt mean and another knew I needed to remain composed. As the person was about to leave the office they gave me their personal email address, phone number and a hug and thanked me for handling the situation the way I did.

This can't go on

Have you ever had one of those moments when you've said to yourself 'I can't do this anymore' or 'something needs to change here'?

I was working as a director in a job that was full-on. I had a lot of responsibility. I often felt isolated. The work was meaningful. I loved the team I was responsible for. There were tensions in the organization, some were easier to navigate than others. For the most part I had constructive working relationships with my colleagues but there was one in particular who I found more and more difficult to work with.

On arrival at the office each morning, a name board would show you who, if anyone, was in before you. One morning as I walked up the stairs, I became aware of myself pretend-retching as I saw that this particular colleague was in the office before me. This was a visceral reaction. If anyone had seen me, they definitely would have asked me what the hell was going on.

I caught myself. I noticed it. I became aware. **It was an 'a-ha' moment**. I vividly remember thinking to myself that it was time to do something about the situation. That what I was doing wasn't healthy. I also realized that this was not the first morning I had done that. Although I didn't necessarily recall doing it previously, it felt familiar.

Being aware of what is going on is often a first step towards change. We often aren't aware of things we do until we become aware of them either by noticing ourselves or being told by someone else. When we become aware we can't not notice them. It is what we do when we become aware that counts.

Why do I have to fake it?

Author and writing coach, Greta Solomon, studied psychology in university and in the space between graduating and her first job she enrolled with a recruitment agency. She attended several interviews. In one of these she was interviewing for an assistant role in an investment bank that would later progress to a banking role. The interview was going well until the interviewer said:

> 'This is what your life is going to be like when you're here. You're going to be working until 9 or 10 at night, every night. You're going to be in a very intense, highly pressured environment. But it's okay we have a pharmacist on site, we have all of these amenities, we have a place where you can get food, so it's absolutely fine.'

She says he painted a very vivid picture for her of what her life was *not* going to be like if she was working there. And when he asked, 'so what do you think?' she replied, 'that just sounds awful'.

Greta says that in her naivety she didn't get that she was supposed to put on a false self at work and instead felt that this wasn't somewhere she wanted to work. She said the interviewer was horrified, shocked, curious and unsure what to say all at the same time. He brought the interview to a close. However, her contact at the agency who was furious with Greta knew exactly what to say. She warned her to never ever do that again; to agree to everything an interviewer says and to tell them that she was perfectly happy with everything.

Greta said she asked herself, 'Why do I have to fake it? Why do I have to pretend that I'm okay?'

Greta feels fortunate that she had that insight at such a young age as many people don't heed what their feelings are communicating at the time but might reach a point where they can no longer cope with not being themselves.[1]

Being yourself

Eamon FitzGerald, founder of WineSpark, joined Naked Wines in his mid 20s. Within a year of being there the founder, Rowan, moved to the US to establish Naked Wines there and asked Eamon to be MD in the UK. Eamon, aged 26 or 27 at the time, says he had 'no experience of running a team, let alone a company'. He believes Rowan must have seen something in him even if he didn't see it in himself. Eamon says one of the greatest things Rowan taught him is to 'value attitude over experience' and acknowledges that Rowan 'could have hired someone a lot older and a lot more experienced than me'. He said there were 35 people, 25,000 customers and £30 million in sales and 'suddenly you're supposed to run the thing'.

Eamon says he didn't get off to a great start as he didn't have a clue what he was doing which he can see now was 'probably quite normal'. **He said, 'it took probably one of the most humiliating experiences of my life to really change gear'.**

He was invited to speak in front of 500 people at a marketing event in London. Being quite introverted, public speaking terrified him. He'd represented Naked Wines at previous events and, although always feeling terrified, they had gone well. Eamon believes the biggest mistake he was making in the early days of being a MD, is a common one – trying to be someone else or the person who did the role before you. And because he didn't have a clue what he was doing he decided the best course of action was to try and be Rowan. Rowan, he says, 'is this charismatic, entrepreneurial, softly spoken South African who set up 3 businesses for Richard Branson of Virgin, created Naked Wines and is just such a presence. Big shoes to fill.'

The speech started well. Then he looked down at the audience and saw someone in the front row who he says, 'just looked bored'. That threw him, he lost his train of thought, his voice began to go dry and then disappeared completely. He said: '[I] just froze on stage in front of 500 people and obviously wanted the stage to swallow me up. I kind of recovered and battled through the last 5 or 6 minutes.' Back at his seat he thought about how awful his speech was. Someone seated near him told him that people loved when he talked about the winemakers. Eamon was appreciative, if sceptical. But after, Eamon said, 'I reflected on that experience and thought there was something in that. I was at my most comfortable talking about the winemakers and their stories rather than the business model and the funding and all that stuff'.

He decided that the next time he was on stage he would focus on the winemakers. And he says those speeches are 'a walk in the park' when he does that.

'As it turns out, being authentically me means more sales when it comes to marketing and everything. So that was a big lesson I learned early on. It took a very tough learning experience, but that sense of being yourself, for all its flaws and all its good things as well, that was a huge learning for me.'[2]

Stepping into the unknown

The very first episode of *Life Beyond the Numbers* is called *Stepping into the Unknown* because of something my guest, Sue Rosen, said during our conversation.

During her career she had thought many times about further study – she loved learning. Sue became aware of a pattern of holding herself back because she was concerned about whether or not there would be any benefit to it – she was doing a cost-benefit analysis on her own learning. **Sometimes we need to step into the unknown rather than always waiting to know what it is we're stepping into'** she said.

We need to do things that interest or engage us even if we are not really sure where that might lead. She said she realized that she wasn't giving herself the freedom to try new things because her head was full of the '*shoulds*':

'I *should* do this. I *should* have a career that looks like this. I *should* work these kinds of hours. I should do this for my family. Oh, also as a working mother, I should be the one who looks after everybody and everything and all those pressures we put on ourselves. Some of them come from other people, but we've absorbed them all.'

During a retreat Sue had what she calls a defining moment when a therapist asked her what her gut was telling her in relation to her career. Her response: 'Hmm, nothing'. She said she had completely lost touch with what she wanted which led her to do some soul-searching including doing more holistic activities and reflection. Sue is always urging people to create the time and space for reflection. Because,

> 'when we are so busy on some little hamster wheel, we lose track of what's really important to us and we lose track of where our energy would be best spent, where we're going to create our energy and how are we going to use it.'[3]

What do you want?

When I spoke with John Collins, he was CFO at Pukka Herbs UK. John, like me, is ex-Deloitte. He had several different roles with Diageo and subsequently left during a restructure. John said that all of the career choices he made up until that point were extrinsically motivated – either by what he thought was the right thing, what he thought others would say was the sensible option or because someone simply suggested an opportunity to him. He has no regrets about his choices but realized that when all the external voices were removed, he was faced with the question, **what does the voice inside say?** He said:

> '…. that was really hard because for a long time it wasn't saying anything to me. Or maybe, I wasn't allowing myself to listen to that voice. What does John the individual want to do? When that question has been answered for you for such a long time that's

really hard. But I do know, ultimately, that listening, and understanding what motivates you intrinsically, is really the key to... this is a bit out there... but I think that's the key to happiness, full stop.'

John can't say when, if ever, he would have chosen for himself or taken control of his own situation. He tells people that losing their jobs opens up opportunities that they never knew existed and means that 'genuinely because I've lived it myself'.[4]

Meaningful work

Career and business coach, Kris Lantheaume, says that from a young age, she learned to find safety in success. Her superpower, she said, is being able to put herself into other people's perspectives and be who they need her to be. In the corporate world this worked well as a strategy. However, as she climbed higher, she needed to know that her time and effort was going towards something that felt meaningful to her. She realized it wasn't and that she had never stopped to figure out what it was that she wanted. She said this made sense to her because of her habit of looking for external validation and defining herself based on what she thought other people wanted.

She made the decision to leave her corporate role to work for herself. When I asked Kris what her definition of success is now, she replied 'trusting myself and being patient enough to see what emerges rather than rushing to create some version of success that makes sense to other people'. And she offered a powerful question for any of us in workplaces to ask: **What can we all do to make this a more engaging and meaningful experience?**[5]

The bottom line: Trust yourself. Listen to yourself. Understand yourself. Be yourself.

7

Accounting for emotions

'Harmony makes small things grow, lack of it makes great things decay.'

Sallust

A snapshot: A further adaption of the personal balance sheet story in Chapter 2.

A bottom-line impact

In many organizations we operate within silos, unaware of the value of leveraging the wisdom and knowledge available. Departments might compete with one another for scarce resources. And some people might intimidate or undermine others intentionally or unintentionally. We leave things unspoken, unexplored and unresolved. This shapes how we relate to one another and has an impact on creativity and innovation.

We are disconnected from ourselves and others. We don't always connect what is going on in our body with the situation we are in, especially when faced with uncertainty or perceived threats. Our internal data may not always be accurate. By tuning into what is going on in our body and revaluing the data we can become more resourceful and distinguish between feeling unsafe or uncomfortable. With a greater sense of self, we can self-regulate, co-regulate and move through complexity, difficulty, tension and uncertainty more confidently.

This applies to you and the person nearest to you as well as every other person on the planet. You might not like my *creative accounting* approach to your life and that's fine too. I am providing an alternative perspective on how we can account for our lives and work out a balance that works best for us. I'm adapting the financial statements, the balance sheet specifically, to present a view of things that impact individual performance. Each person impacts the performance of the organization so our cumulative physical, mental and emotional states can all have an impact on the bottom line. Our brain and body are always working to keep us in balance. **Are you optimally balanced? Do you feel resourced to live and work as your best self?**

Budgeting

It seems sensible, reasonable, logical even that the healthier we are and the better we look after our own bodies then the better our body-budgeting works. If our systems are all working as they are designed to do our brains have more capacity to do other things, like be creative, innovative and collaborative. If our brain is (re)deploying resources to compensate for less-than-optimal resource management does this mean that we are less resourced to do our best work? The more aware we are of what supplies our energy and what depletes us of energy, the better our lives could be. When we feel resourced this can also have a ripple effect on people we come in contact with.

Body-budgeting is predictive. It is future focused. In the same way an organizational budget is future focused. It is a plan of action in numbers. We compare the budget to actual and explain variances but that isn't the same as reflecting on, and understanding, the results. We need to stand back and look at the bigger picture, the long-term view. What is the impact to the balance sheet? Short-term corrective measures to the budget, like having a quick coffee or stepping outside for a smoke, might impede a long-term strategic view of maintaining an optimally proportioned balance.

A physical balance sheet

Imagine when you show up for work each day that you are a physical manifestation of your balance sheet – a snapshot without the details. On the face of it you and your team members have a balanced balance sheet. When you meet a member of your team is it obvious to you how their body budget is proportioned? While the debits might equal the credits how are the proportions within in and between? A balance sheet is always in balance but how our balance sheets compare depend on how we manage our resources?

Each of us requires certain daily essentials to enable us to get through our day. For example, we need a recommended amount of sleep, a nutritionally optimal diet, to remain hydrated and to exercise. If Sam turns up at work regularly smiling widely and looking healthy but is either under slept or dehydrated, for example, would you know? Would you be aware of the impact this might have on Sam's performance? Is Sam?

> 'The science is crystal clear on healthful food, regular exercise, and sleep as prerequisites for a balanced body budget and a healthy emotional life. A chronically taxed body budget increases your chances of developing a host of different illnesses.'
>
> Lisa Feldman Barrett[1]

Throughout our lives we expend and earn energy. We make both energy profits and energy losses. We expend energy each time we think, feel or do. Some of the activities that we earn energy from are also activities we expend energy on – when we sleep, eat and exercise, for example.

Energy earnings > Energy expenditure = Profit
Energy earnings < Energy expenditure = Loss

Why do we sleep?

Sleep is vital to our day-to-day wellbeing. If you are painting a wall and you only apply one coat of paint the wall might look fine, but it won't look its best. When you apply a second coat that makes all the difference. That completes it and makes it more durable. You needed both coats. Adequate sleep is like having 2 coats of paint – you are ready for the world; you are more resilient. Without adequate sleep you'll get by but never as your best self.

As adults we need between 7 and 9 hours of sleep. If we are not getting adequate sleep, and if that becomes our norm, that has all sorts of body-budgeting implications. In *Why We Sleep*, Matthew Walker explains that scientific research conducted over 60 years does not support the idea that people can function well on only 4 or 5 hours of sleep per night. He warns that when we are sleep deprived, we are unable to tell how sleep deprived we are.

'With chronic sleep restriction over months or years, an individual will actually acclimate to their impaired performance, lower alertness, and reduced energy levels. That low-level exhaustion becomes their accepted norm, or baseline. Individuals fail to recognize how their perennial state of sleep deficiency has come to compromise their mental aptitude and physical vitality, including the slow accumulation of ill health. A link between the former and latter is rarely made in their mind.'[2]

We expend energy when we sleep as our brain processes our learning and keeps the systems of our body running. We also earn energy as we sleep. Imagine that the energy earnings from sleep sit in our energy account on the balance sheet and we can withdraw that energy to match expenditure needs throughout the day. This it isn't a savings account though as the sleep balance resets daily. If we sleep more than the required amount there isn't any additional earnings other than perhaps the enjoyment of extra sleep. We are designed with an inbuilt sleep system.

What happens when we don't get the required amount of sleep? We may not have had a proper restorative sleep and so we earn less energy than we need for the next day to be at our best. Perhaps we missed out on processing all of our learning, meaning that we wasted some of the previous days precious resources. We might have to relearn it at a later date, incurring an additional expense. We also incur a metabolic tax which becomes a liability – something we will owe later. Over time if we don't get adequate sleep our immune system can become run down making us ill. This will put a strain on our body-budgeting as it is costly to recover. We might reduce some of our metabolic tax liability as we recover.

Example

When Sam and Alex show up to work every day, they appear the same outwardly. You don't spend a lot of time with them and don't know much about them but most days you see them at their desks putting in the hours. What you don't see is the proportions that make up their balance, the details. You don't see how much sleep they had for example.

Take a look at Chart 7.

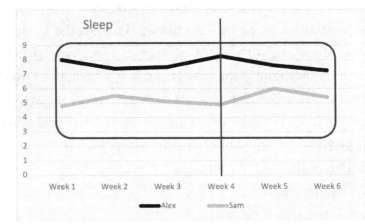

Chart 7 Sleep

Alex sleeps on average between 7 and 8 hours a night. Alex is prepared for the workday.

Sam, on the other hand, rarely gets 7 hours sleep. Sam has a diminished capacity to work at their best. Sam might not be aware of this because this day-to-day routine is *normal* for them. They have adjusted to sleeping less. They are unaware that their body budget has to compensate for a sleep deficit. None of us will immediately be aware of amount of sleep that they had.

The line at Week 4 represents one particular week at work where both Sam and Alex are involved in a critical piece of work that will influence the future direction of the organization and involve some key decisions. Who, in your opinion, will be more optimally resourced to undertake this work at their best?

Food glorious food

Next are our nutritional needs – what we eat and drink. All of us have basic nutritional needs. They impact our performance levels too – our food fuels our performance. If we eat the right proportion of food types and absorb the right proportion of nutrients into our system as well as maintain a healthy gut, it goes a long way towards living well. The nutrients each of us needs varies between us, within us and at different stages in our lives. It is a vast topic and way too detailed to venture into here. We need to eat well. We need to keep hydrated. The better we do both of those things the better our body will feel and perform.

Take a look at Chart 8.

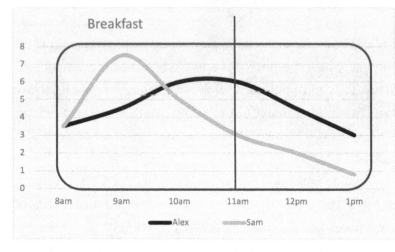

Chart 8 Breakfast

Most days Alex eats oats for breakfast, knowing that this maintains fairly consistent energy levels throughout the morning.

Sam prefers a big bowl of sugary cereal for breakfast and feels the benefit of that sugar boost when the working day starts. However, it wears off relatively quickly further diminishing their capacity to perform at their best.

The line at 11am represents a negotiation meeting with a key supplier. Who, in your opinion, will be more optimally resourced to negotiate at their best?

Sleep and breakfast are only 2 factors. How many more are there to consider? And if you overlay them all on top of one another what impact would it have on their performance and the performance of the organization? And then consider the cumulative balance sheets of everyone in your team, department and organization.

What about emotions and feelings?

Let's start with engagement. Take a look at Chart 9.

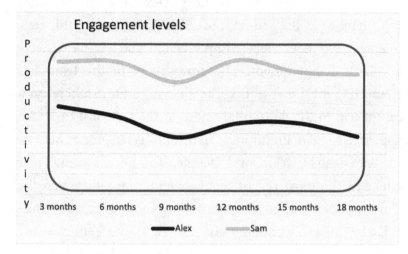

Chart 9 Engagement levels

Sam is hugely engaged at work. They expend energy throughout the day and are also earning energy as they feel engaged, satisfied, motivated, appreciated and valued. Overall, Sam finds work fulfilling and makes an annual engagement profit. The dividends from these retained earnings will sustain Sam in future in the case of a sudden change in factors that influence these engagement levels.

How much more productive would Sam be if they maintained a more optimal physical balance?

Alex is slightly disengaged at work. They tend to expend more energy than they earn. This is taking a toll, and a metabolic tax is beginning to build up in their liabilities on their balance sheet.

Changes at work

Alex is a considered a high performer and recently began reporting into a new line manager. Alex's new line manager is a member of the senior leadership team. So far, this new manager has been very unpredictable and seems to have a volatile temperament. The atmosphere in the team has changed. Sam didn't notice the change in atmosphere on a recent trip to the department and on the face of it the team appeared to be maintaining a harmonious balance as before.

Alex leads a team of 8 people. The new line manager attended the most recent team meeting and addressed the team in a demanding and controlling tone. Alex was blind-sided by this and wondered how the team were feeling during the meeting as Alex felt a little intimidated and fearful of what was being said and how it was being said.

Chart 10 represents how Alex's team members felt during the 1-hour meeting.

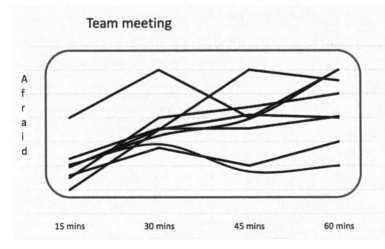

Chart 10 Team meeting

Everyone appeared to agree with what was being discussed and it wasn't obvious from how people looked what was happening on the inside, what they were thinking or feeling. Nobody felt in a position to disagree with some of the proposals that were being put forward about returning to the office. They didn't believe that their voice would count.

Alex goes back to their office and goes through the meeting over and over in their head. Ruminating is exhausting and can expend energy, as well as distract those who are engaged at work from being fully engaged at work. Alex is masterful at masking this tendency and from the outside you don't know what is going on. The rumination can last for days depending on how close to the bone it feels.

It is easy to see how 8 team members will have 8 different understandings and views on what went on in that meeting. What will the result be? How will it impact stress levels amongst and between them?

What happens when we are stressed?

Stress mobilizes our body's resources to help us cope with threats, and that's a good thing. We need moderate amounts of stress to work, to play sports, to learn. We really wouldn't manage without it. But our body also needs time to rest and recover. There is always a balancing act. In Chapter 4 we talked about the importance of body-budgeting. Incidents of acute stress are manageable, we can ramp it up, deal with whatever's in front of us, and then recover and restore. However, an above normal rate of stress can turn into chronic stress. Chronic stress is a completely different story. Teetering on the brink of chronic stress is probably not far off where many of us spend our lives.

Chronic stress impacts both body and brain and our body-budgeting. As long as we are in a state of chronic stress our brain will budget for emergency measures and our body will keep up the supply to meet the demand. However, our body may not be able to use the full supply and that comes with penalties or fines in the form of extra costs and metabolic taxes. These costs and metabolic taxes can result in an increase in immune system suppression, digestive disruption, rising blood sugar levels, weight gain and damaged blood vessels and heart. If you would like to know what stress does to your brain, I encourage you to watch Dr Lara Boyd's captivating TEDx talk *How can stress affect learning?*[3]

Which rocks first, the chicken or the egg?

Would you recognize a state of chronic stress? In yourself or in others? As I write this, the temperature is high. It's 25°C (77°F) inside and hotter outside. Sudden changes in temperature are not unheard of. When it rises or drops slowly, we tend to adapt more easily, but a sudden increase can be harder to adjust to. In December 2022, I can remember arriving home after being away for a few days. We had left the heating off while away and our house was so cold, less than 10°C (50°F) degrees. For a few hours it was a struggle to adapt. The only option was to go to bed with layers of clothing on, a hat, 2 duvets and chattering teeth.

But amazingly, as we've seen, our body has inbuilt systems to help it adapt. I look back on my own work-life and how the temperature of stress was gradually rising, and I didn't always realize how hot it was. At times the temperature rose in an unmanageable way.

The normal stresses of life

The World Health Organization categorizes good mental health as being able to cope with the normal stresses of life, work productively, realize your potential and contribute to your community.[4]

The normal stresses of life – how do you define those? What is normal for me might not be for you.

A stressful job

I think of myself as mentally strong, mentally healthy, mentally fit, mentally resilient. Whatever phrase you want to use, I am one of those glass half-full, even maybe a little bit more, type people. I count myself fortunate that I don't typically worry. I rarely feel anxious. And I believe I can take on a fair amount of responsibility without feeling overwhelmed or stressed. Most importantly, I feel normal. I am normal. For me at least. I don't know any different. I only know my own experiences, my own thoughts, my own feelings.

When I felt stressed at work, I accepted a certain level of stress as normal, and over time my stress appetite or tolerance level expanded. Of course, this level couldn't increase indefinitely. At some point my body reacted. What was the cost of this, short term and long term? Sometimes I got ill and would be off work. I saw my holidays as an opportunity for recovery. Holidays are meant for enjoyment, not for recovery.

We talk about empathy and putting ourselves in other people's shoes. But it's next to impossible to imagine what it is actually like to be someone else. Because no matter how hard we try to imagine what it is like for them, we are imagining their experience through our own lens.

How often do we stop and think about our own lives from our perspective and ask is what we have normalized actually normal?

How do we know for definite that we are coping, or we are stressed?

What is the cumulative impact of stress on our lives?

When you start a new job, your balance sheet might look quite different than it will 6 months later.

- You're prepared for a loss in the beginning because you're going to invest in learning and you're going to expend physical and mental energy getting to know people.
- There might be a steep learning curve if it is a step up or a new industry. Of course, you invest willingly as you expect a return on that investment in terms of new challenges, new collaborations, engagement and satisfaction.
- You know that there will be body-budgeting consequences, but a short-term investment and loss should rebalance and generate dividends in the longer-term. It seems like a wise investment of your resources.

Your balance sheet might look something like Chart 11 over the first 6 months.

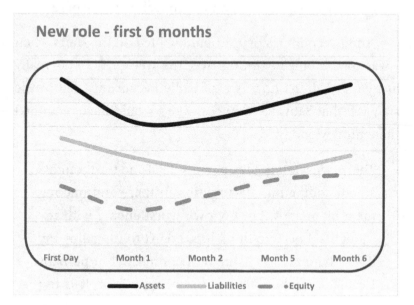

Chart 11 New role – first 6 months

Below are excerpts from personal emails that I sent to friends over a 3–4-year period in my first director role. The first email was sent 3 months in the role.

As you read through these be curious as to whether you think that I was mentally healthy, mentally fit, mentally resilient or mentally strong.

There's so much work to be done. It is really daunting, and although I keep convincing myself, it is all achievable. I go through days of despair.

Life is hectic. It's going well, but it's way more demanding and challenging than I expected.

Life is incredibly hectic here. I'm just working all the time, even most Saturdays and some Sundays. I am really stressed actually, and I can feel it everywhere.

And I recount a story about how I fell on the stairs when I was in the office working over the weekend. I was really lucky that I didn't hurt myself badly because if I fell in the stairwell that Saturday chances were I would have remained there until Monday.

There is just lots going on in my head and the thoughts are all competing for attention in there and making me a bit snappy. I'm my own worst enemy with my thoughts. I need to think less. I don't think telling my boss I hate my job is the best approach, but perhaps I can tell my boss that I am unhappy in it. It is too stressful and erratic, and I just can't see a long-term future. Or is that a risky strategy? I feel that I have become what I do and not who I am.

Stress levels are very high. There is a building being renovated across from the office, and there has been constant drilling for the last 5 weeks. I'm getting headaches every day, but I can't figure out if it is just the drilling or just the work stress or a combination of both.

Very busy, more than I ever really imagined. I'm not even here a year yet and feel like it has been about 5. I think most of the reasons I left Africa have just followed me here, and so I haven't managed to get the whole work–life balance worked out yet. I enjoy my job most of the time, but it is consuming me and so not really sustainable, I think.

I think I bit off more than I can chew. Work is tough going, and I'm feeling the pressure.

Not sure how long more I'll stay. I need a job that is not so demanding and gives me a bit more of a work–life balance or even more of a life.

I rarely leave the office for lunch and usually eat at my desk. I've worked 60 days overtime this year. I'm self-motivated, but this is clearly not sustainable or healthy. I've been covering a gap that needs to be addressed.

Being a director is no joke. The responsibility is so stressful. I have so many sleepless nights. It is also an amazing organization and I love what we do. The impact makes it worth it, I guess.

Sad to see a colleague go and also jealous that my colleague has managed to get out.

After 3 years when I was on holidays I had a massage and the masseuse told me my shoulders were rock hard, at a dangerous level. I didn't take much notice as rock hard shoulders were normal for me. On my first day back over lunch one of my direct reports said something like 'Susan, you looked absolutely great this morning, but now you look haggard.' And he went on to say, 'I hate to use that word because it's a horrible way to describe anyone, but I need to tell you'. **That was a wakeup call.**

I was unaware of what I was doing to myself. On some level I knew – you can infer that from the emails – but what was I doing about it? Justifying it to myself. I was not aware of the level of stress and perhaps the damage that I was doing to myself. Not long after that holiday I handed in my notice, and I left. I left feeling quite hurt, disappointed and upset. And I carried feelings of anger and animosity for quite some time after that. I believed I'd been undermined and bullied. The stress wasn't caused by workload alone.

I imagine that my balance sheet looked like Chart 12 over the 3-year period.

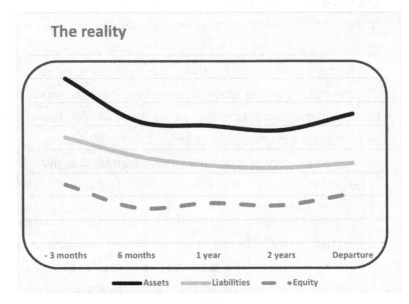

Chart 12 The reality

Remember the section on going concern in Chapter 1? I was effectively giving myself a clean audit opinion every year and telling the world that going concern was not an issue. It was though.

Stress had taken a toll on me and increased my metabolic tax liability. Stress had become my normal; that doesn't mean it was helpful or healthy for my assets including my brain and body and energy*flow*. I was incurring losses annually, eroding my equity, and losing part of my identity as I lost sight of what mattered most to me.

Keep stressed and carry on

We might think of the opposite of health as ill health or poor health. But many of us might normalize our unhealthy levels of stress. We grin and bear it. It is what it is. I believed at the time that I was coping with my stress levels, the workload, the responsibilities. Now I wonder how much better a job I could have done if I had been at my best? How much better of a job could I have done if I was fully supported? How much better of a job could I have done if I had challenged some of the toxic work practices?

I've only got my own experience to go on. As health and wellbeing are talked about more openly now it often amazes me how it can be approached from the individual side, like it's an individual issue only. But it's complex and influenced by individual, environmental and social factors. Individual factors include our genetics, personality and life experiences. They affect how we think, feel, and act. They help determine how we handle stress, relate to others, make choices and decisions.

There are things happening in workplaces that contribute to this that I don't think we always know how to deal with, like micromanagement, bullying and harassment. What role do these factors play in undermining a working environment that promotes sustainable health and wellbeing? If we are in an organization where we have inadequate support, or no support, or stress is really high, or the workload is really high, or the environment is toxic, all of those things contribute to not coping with the *normal* stresses of daily life, not being productive and not realizing your potential.

Today I can ask what role I played in all of that. I'm not sure that I had that level of awareness or emotional maturity or self-reflection then to be able to take a step back and look at what was really going on. But when we are fully immersed in a situation it is difficult to judge – when you're in the bottle, you can't read the label. It is not always easy to take an honest look at yourself and what you are contributing to the situation you're in. And we tend to assign blame to other people and to blame the situation and blame the circumstances, but we have a responsibility to see our part in it. It isn't to say that the situation wasn't stressful.

If I asked you to tell me *honestly* how much stress you are under. What would you say?

Is it a normal level? Or is it normal *for you*?

A strategy

Would you recommend living like this as a strategy? The pressure of an always-on culture helps us to override our basic needs, but at what cost? Are we wilfully trading our energy, our own sustainability, for success in the short-term.

Are we maximizing our productivity to the detriment of our health and wellbeing?

Are we fooling ourselves that we are maximizing our productivity and performance by pushing and being constantly on?

We can't possibly be working at our best if our body and brain aren't feeling at their best. Even if we think we are.

Perhaps the health and wellbeing of people is more inextricably linked with that of our organizations than we realize. When we are all in the same boat there is something strangely reassuring about that. We're all in this together. No need to rock the boat.

What can you do to generate a different result?

Your wellbeing

The Science of Wellbeing, taught by Laurie Santos, is the most popular class in Yale University's history.[5] This course exposes many of the outdated beliefs in circulation about what makes us happy and takes you through strategies that you can cultivate to improve your wellbeing. You can enrol online for free. If you do, one of the first things you learn about is the simple act of savouring.

Savouring is consciously delighting in or relishing an experience so that you appreciate it. It can be a mood booster as it gets us to focus on what is meaningful to us about the experience, keeps us present when we are in the experience and can increase feelings of gratitude. I like to make these experiences multi-sensorial – include the sounds, smells and tastes as well as what you were feeling. The beauty is in the details, the intricacies, the moments.

And later, much later, you can bring that experience to mind and almost transport yourself to that exact moment and conjure up those feelings again. Or when you notice a smell or hear a sound that too will transport you. Take a moment now and bring to mind a favourite meal or night out with friends or place you visited. Go into the details and notice how you can change the way you feel. Experience the joy.

This isn't about thinking positive or being blissfully happy every day or savouring experiences that are difficult for you. This is about appreciating the little things, making more of moments, making moments meaningful and rather than chasing happiness or chasing joy begin to actively cultivate them. Make space, create time to 'stand and stare'. An unpleasant experience can cost us even when we are no longer in the situation and a pleasant one can continue to pay us dividends for years simply by bringing it to mind and savouring it. As we have seen both can change your mood.

Have some fun

When the last time you laughed aloud? Or laughed for no reason? We are all born with the ability to laugh. It is one of our body's natural ways of releasing tension. It can change how we react and give us pause to reconsider our response. It can be contagious. A moment infused with laughter can feel like medicine. Laughing together, at work, is a great way of connecting with others.

Life is serious, work is serious, but do we always have to take everything so seriously? We don't have to be serious all the time to be taken seriously. I'm not advocating for undermining the urgency of what you do or to make light of it. Rather I'm asking you to consider where you can afford to take a more light-hearted approach and profit from some of the many benefits of laughter, like:

- building resilience;
- boosting your immune system; and
- massaging and invigorating your insides (*gut*).

Humour is one of my top 3 strengths and in all seriousness if I don't infuse some fun, humour and laughter in my day, the cracks begin to show. We all have the ability to proactively cultivate moments of laughter in our lives. We can start by learning to laugh at ourselves.

Know your rhythm

Our circadian rhythm is a 24-hour cycle. Within that 24-hour cycle our ultradian rhythms represent recurring biological rhythms. Although I've read and heard about the benefits to focus and performance by adhering to this rhythm several times, I never paid proper attention to it. Until this year when a cherished mentor, Clay, (re)introduced me to it. Hand on heart it was a game changer when it came to writing this book. I was able to restore my energy and perform at a consistent level.

In *The Power of Full Engagement*, Jim Loehr and Tony Schwartz explain our ultradian rhythms really well:

'These ultradian rhythms help to account for the ebb and flow of energy throughout the day. Physiological measures such as heart rate, hormonal levels, muscle tension and brain-wave activity all increase during the first part of the cycle – and so does alertness. After an hour or so, these measures start to decline.

Somewhere between 90 and 120 minutes, the body begins to crave a period of rest and recovery. Signals include a desire to yawn and stretch, hunger pangs, increased tension, difficulty concentrating, an inclination to procrastinate or fantasize, and a higher incidence of mistakes. We are capable of over-riding these natural cycles, but only summoning the fight or flight response and flooding our bodies with stress hormones that are designed to help us handle emergencies.'[6]

The final piece brings the Performance Paradox covered in Chapter 4 to mind. I highly recommend experimenting with this 90–120-minute activity-rest cycle. The key is an active recovery period. Scrolling on your phone or watching TV is passive. Active means to actively do something else – I did all sorts – yoga, sewing, meditation, swimming, picking blackberries, strolling, running and more.

Motion is lotion

Movement is crucial to our wellbeing.

Our lifestyles can be sedentary. We instinctively know when we need *to get some air* or *some space* or *a walk to clear our head*.

When we move, we use different muscles, we sense different things, our brain shifts its focus from what we were doing to what we are doing. We can continue to think in the background. Stimulating different senses helps us make new connections and consider different perspectives. Movement is like medicine.

The World Health Organization recommends at least 2.5 hours of moderate exercise a week, or a minimum of 21 minutes per day. WHO also suggests we should aim to do more than the minimum recommendations to limit the amount of time we spend sitting (at a desk) which has a negative impact on our health.[7]

When it comes to exercise, it can be hard to know where to start. We often start out with setting an ambitious goal like running a marathon, completing a triathlon or climbing Kilimanjaro. Momentum can be difficult to sustain if the stretch is a bit too much. I love a challenge, but I also realize I get a great return on investment by exercising consistently. Give yourself permission to start small and remember: **'The best exercise is exercise you are going to do.'**[8]

Stand and stare

'We have no time to stand and stare' is a line from the poem *Leisure* by Welsh poet W. H. Davies.

We can actively slow down and the benefits to slowing down are numerous, including mental and physical well-being, increased focus and creativity, and creating time for important things.

Professor Giana M. Eckhardt of King's College London studies people's desire to slow down or decelerate. Deceleration, she says, involves 3 elements:

1. Embodied deceleration is a form of active slowing down, like walking or doing yoga.
2. Technological deceleration involves feeling in control of technology rather than feeling controlled by it.
3. Episodic deceleration involves engaging in fewer daily actions and making fewer choices.

When I asked Giana about whether slowing down would factor in the workplace, she said she thinks companies are starting to realize that this is something they need to support people with but are not exactly sure what to do. She did highlight Craigberoch Decelerator Lab on the Isle of Bute. The founder, Gib Bulloch, envisions companies sending teams there to learn different ways of slowing down. This will enable them learn the importance of creating space to tap into their creativity in order to tackle bigger issues rather than always being bogged down by busyness[9]. We'll meet Gib in the next chapter.

Personal balance sheet

Consider what you would put into your balance sheet with this starter checklist:

- How do you manage your energy*flow*?
- What matters most to you and are you building your equity with this?
- What, or who, drains your resources and replenishes them?
- Do you know how to value your intangibles – strengths, values?

- Are you aware of metabolic taxes you pay when you feel discomfort or tension or are under slept?
- What is the return on investment of maintaining an optimal level of health?
- What is the impact of cumulative losses?
- Are you trying to generate profit at any cost?
- What is your unique formula?

The bottom line: Take account of your whole self and take your whole self into account.

Part 4

Business sense and sensibility

8

Disintegration and dysregulation: regulation and integration

'It is not because things are difficult that we do not dare, it is because we do not dare that they are difficult.'

Seneca

A snapshot: Organizational culture is a complex accumulation, interaction and interconnection of personal balance sheets.

A corporate body

You might have come across the term 'body corporate' – so let's play with that term as a metaphor for all organizations and compare a corporate body and a human body. You could have some fun with this and use different body parts like heart, soul, limbs or gut to represent different teams or departments. For now, imagine the leadership team are the brain and the rest of the organization is the body.

The leadership team, as the brains of the operation, are in the dark. They depend upon the information flow from their senses.

- How much attention do they pay to that information?
- How do they interpret it?
- Do they prefer to do what they've always done because their neural pathways are strong?

Perhaps they value the brain over the rest of the body and take the body for granted. They disregard the data, suppress it, misinterpret it or override it. It falls on deaf ears.

What about when something goes wrong?

- Do they acknowledge that they have made a prediction error, or is the body to blame? A broken limb, weak heart or troubled gut.
- Maybe they think the body is slowing them down and they could replace parts of it or just dispense of some altogether.
- They hold the head up high. While they get that the body has its uses, they just don't seem to grasp that a whole healthy body is of greater value than the sum of its parts.

Any ailment, infection or illness in the body will impact the brain too. They may act as though they are disembodied in their delusion of being headstrong. *Off with their heads* isn't the answer either. Will the brain survive without the body?

The whole is greater than the sum of the parts

Organizational culture is a set of shared values, beliefs, attitudes and assumptions. It is a proxy for the emotional state of an organization, or the collective emotional states of people who work there. People in leadership positions exert influence over this. Emotional contagion is present at work as moods and feelings can synchronize, spread and impact performance. Our nervous systems are always communicating, and we can co-regulate. It's our loss when we don't acknowledge this on an organizational level.

Disengagement is a costly problem. It has reached epidemic proportions. On a daily basis people make decisions and take actions that affect the bottom line. These will be influenced by factors like what motivates them, how they feel about themselves, whether they feel valued and feel a sense of belonging. How people feel about their colleagues, manager, leadership and organization also count. **Why are we perpetuating cultures that fail to engage more than 1 in 5 people?**

The financial statements are a set of reports that can be used to analyze an organization's financial health, position and performance. There is a direct relationship between people's performance and the performance of the organization. In Chapter 1 we saw how the true financial health of some organizations might well have presented a real account of organizational health. And in Chapter 7 we looked at individuals and how they show up at work influences their working day. How can we profit from accounting for our emotions?

Do you know 'what tangible difference an employee who feels engaged makes to performance over one that feels disengaged?'[1]

Conditions at work

There is a clear business case for focusing on engagement in the workplace. When people are engaged at work, they are more efficient and productive, there is better morale, retention, customer service and overall performance. The focus needs to be on changing the conditions people work in, not the people. Root causes of workplace disengagement must be put under the spotlight. What are you doing to create conditions for people to feel engaged?

A 2020 Global Workplace Study reported that people who felt that they belonged to a team were twice as likely to be fully engaged. Furthermore, they found that when team members felt that they fully trusted their team leader, they were 12 times more likely to be fully engaged at work.[2]

Finding ways to help people feel engaged at work includes understanding the feelings people have toward themselves, their work and their colleagues. Feelings have for too long been ignored. It is time to welcome them in, to understand them and to create environments that encourage feelings of engagement.

Sick building syndrome[3]

During my Deloitte days I remember hearing about a building that had been designated a 'sick building'. 'Sick building syndrome' resulted in reduced productivity, increased absenteeism and even some strikes in certain Irish workplaces in the 1970s and 80s. It was not a uniquely Irish phenomenon. The condition included symptoms such as respiratory issues, headaches and fatigue. One cause seemed to be the lack of autonomy people had over the ventilation in their work environment. People became physically ill, and action was taken to improve the work environment.

Today many of our workplaces are unhealthy. There is a disconnect between how we deal with the physical and psychological. Both impact productivity. Although we don't physically see how people feel about their work, this intangible is tangibly visible in the numbers.

Corporate immune system

Former founding partner and executive director of Accenture Development Partners (ADP), Gib Bulloch, spoke with me about the need to look at the mental health of the organization and the mental health of the system, which is causing mental health problems. He believes the short-term focus needs to be tackled and that organizations can continue to make money with a longer-term perspective.

He says businesses are fairly unhappy places for people to be in at present. As organizations are increasingly faced with an identity crisis, without role models for younger people to emulate, he says the response seems to be: 'Oh, we'll make our workplaces happier places with playgrounds, football in the canteens, fruit on the desks and gym memberships'. This is a nice to have but doesn't get to the heart of the matter.

Instead, Gib recommends that 'people at the highest levels, at all levels, take a long hard look in the mirror and say: What are we here for? What could we do to make the world a better place? Why do we exist? Why is it we're making these [products] that we make and how is it we're going to make them?'

Gib believes that as long as we continue with *business as usual*, we will continue to see unhappy people and people with mental health issues in workplaces. He also says that these symptoms are perfectly normal responses by perfectly normal, healthy human beings who are simply trying to do their best.

ADP scaled massively in its first 10 years. They worked with large non-governmental organizations in 90 countries and provided a quarter billion worth of services. It employed thousands of Accenture staff who, while working with ADP, worked on half-salary but 'were more motivated than ever'. Gib acknowledges that remaining within Accenture, rather than leaving to establish a separate business, enabled ADP to scale more rapidly. He believed by staying he could try to change the business from within. Leadership loved what he was doing, supported, applauded and promoted him.

He said for a long time he was the happiest person, had the best job and was leading a brilliant team of people. But over time they found it harder to break 'the corporate immune system' which Gib says:

'... exists in many companies from what I hear. And it is the invisible forces of middle management, doing their job in fulfilling the rules, enforcing policy, performance management processes that are fit for rewarding usual behaviours rather than incentivising new kinds of behaviours that are needed.

When you are the lightning rod for these, you are the intrapreneur, you get a lot of the credit when things go well ... but then when things don't go so well, the buck stops with you. I found it harder and more difficult. I didn't realise the hours that I was working, because I was so committed to the cause. Eventually I was the one that broke.'

To find out if he broke down or broke through read his book or listen to our podcast episode. Gib's identity was constructed around being Executive Director of ADP. That is who he was. When he left, he spent time unravelling who he was when he was not the business card.[4]

- Are your organizational systems fit for purpose? What purpose?
- Do you know what impact your work environment has on your wellbeing?
- Do you know who you are without your job title?

Dysfunctional or dysregulated?

The term dysfunctional is often used to describe an organization, department, team and even people. The collective terms referred to just describe people coming together in a structured way. Thinking of people as being dysfunctional undermines their humanity. Systems and structures can be dysfunctional. These are built by people and so they can be reimagined and rebuilt.

When we wonder why people aren't behaving in ways that we imagined they would it might be better to think of them, and us, as dysregulated instead of dysfunctional. Each and every one of us has a nervous system which goes in and out of a regulated state – it is a perfectly normal response to navigating the world.

How do we take this into account in our organizations?

I believe that I am privileged to have spent time in workplaces in many countries around the world. I have worked with incredibly talented and inspiring individuals as well as with plenty I would have said were disgruntled and disruptive. I've no doubt the people I worked with said the same about me. One line manager even told me I had a style they never encountered before – I took it as a compliment.

With hindsight I understand the role that a dysregulated nervous system played. Mine and others. We can also be mistaken that other people's behaviour is related to ours. Oftentimes behaviour or actions are as a result of protective mechanisms that no longer serve us. When someone seems angry with you, and you think to yourself 'what did I do?'. Consider the possibility that they are not angry with you but instead might be feeling defensive or insecure.

Some of my colleagues were absolutely in the right roles, and their work brought out the best in them as well as the people around them. Many were not suited to the role they were in, which often brought out the worst in them as well as having a knock-on impact on those around them. There were those whose strengths were unnoticed, or they were taken for granted as well as those who were constantly chipped away at to fit a mould, not shine, or at least outshine their colleagues.

I spent many hours, days and weeks in pointless meetings and workshops where nothing moved forward. I was also fortunate enough to be part of great changes, progress and to make and enact changes. But time and time again I witnessed colleagues not saying what they were thinking, holding back, denying themselves and the world their insights and ideas. Too many were disillusioned, underutilized, unrecognized and undervalued. One colleague's advice to me on their departure was to 'stay as long as you have a voice'. **What is the cost of this silence?**

Keep quiet and carry on

Many people don't think that their voice counts and as a result so much is left unsaid. We sidestep or talk around issues or assume other people understand what we mean even if we don't say it. When we hold back from saying what needs to be said it can eat away at us. This can result in us avoiding the topic or the person or even the work.

Does your voice count?

I've always been one to speak up and to speak out. It got me into trouble, often. That rarely stopped me. Although, I learnt, mostly, when to speak and when to keep quiet. I often felt compelled to speak for people who felt unable to use their own voice. None of us deserves to be silenced. Our voice matters.

Voice is a critical part of effective communication. We don't need a loud voice to be heard. We only need to use it.

Our voice is a gift, a gift to make use of and not to take for granted. My sister, Aoife, never spoke a single word in her 33 years of life. Some of my most stressful times were when I felt I didn't have a voice. Of course, I always had a voice but at times it felt like nobody was listening, interested, cared or understood. Or maybe they simply didn't like what I had to say. Everyone has a voice. Use yours. Let others use theirs.

In October 2018, a brand new 737 MAX-8 plane left Jakarta, Indonesia and within 13 minutes of taking off plunged into the sea killing all 189 people onboard. In March 2019, 157 people died when another 737 MAX-8 plane crashed only 6 minutes after departing Addis Ababa, Ethiopia. A U.S. Senate Committee Report stated that, amongst other things, there was undue pressure on the line engineers and the production staff and that early warnings from Boeing engineers were ignored.[5] This was a price too high to pay. **Could the cost of human lives have been avoided if people's voices were listened to?**

Psychological safety

Amy Edmondson defines team psychological safety as 'a belief that one will not be punished or humiliated for speaking up with ideas, questions, concerns, or mistakes, and that the team is safe for interpersonal risk-taking'. In her TEDx talk, *Building a Psychologically Safe Workplace*, she offers 3 simple steps to foster team psychological safety:

1. To create a rationale for speaking up frame the work as a learning problem and not an execution problem. Make uncertainty and interconnectedness explicit.
2. To creates more safety for speaking up acknowledge your own fallibility.
3. To create a necessity for voice. Model curiosity and ask lots of questions.

Is there psychological safety in your team? How do you know? Because you tell people there is, or others tell you that there is or because you feel there is?

Remember that we *feel* safe. Thinking it is psychologically safe or saying it is psychologically safe is very different to feeling that it is. Unless people FEEL psychologically safe then announcing that a team, department or organization is psychologically safe is simply words and wishes. Amy Edmondson has created a questionnaire that you can use to measure your team's level of psychological safety.[6]

Researchers at Google undertook Project Aristotle to answer the question: 'What are the conditions that enable an effective team?'. The researchers identified 5 key elements of effective teams with psychological safety being the most crucial. The other 4 were mutual trust, structure and clarity, meaning of work and impact.[7]

This is a safe space

We hear this all the time. I use this phrase myself. But just because we declare a space safe it doesn't mean that everyone feels safe.

We don't create feelings of belonging, respect or safety in our organizations by talking about them. We need to walk the talk. We will only feel safe in relationship to others if our nervous system feels safe. We will be scanning the environment for signs of safety as well as signs of danger. We can co-regulate in safety.

Cues of safety include smiling, head nodding, a welcoming tone of voice, being listened to and open body language.

Sitting with your arms folded, with a scowl and announcing to the room in no uncertain terms that this is a safe space can emit cues of danger, even if unintentional.

Nervous systems finely attune to the environment, and we will make meaning based on how we are feeling. It is possible that everyone in the room feels safe and possible that this can change in an instant.

A cue of danger that I recognize in my nervous system is when someone is visibly distracted when they are speaking with me. I feel my heart rate quicken. Another danger signal for me is rising noise levels, in particular mechanical sounds. Have you been thinking about yours?

Is there a difference between feeling unsafe and feeling uncomfortable?

Yes. Absolutely.

Think about it for a moment. What sensations do you associate with feeling unsafe? With feeling uncomfortable? Attune to these sensations. Learn how to discern between them. The more you begin to tune into your inner sensations and delve into the account that your brain presents you the more you can discern the difference between these states.

The conditions, environment or culture at work should be conducive to everyone doing their best work. People should never feel scared or threatened at work. They should not be made to feel afraid at work. While we are responsible for how we feel, if the environment we are in is threatening and full of cues of danger then it seems inevitable that we will feel that fear. Fear spreads. I have certainly worked in environments where the conditions were conducive to competing with one another rather than collaborating, to being dominated and dictated to rather than being treated as an equal.

If the culture of the organization is healthy some people might still experience fear, their own fear in response to an event. We cannot eliminate feelings of fear or anxiety completely, but we can do better at tackling underlying causes of disengagement.

Our old paradigms and models are disintegrating. We can see how organizations are full of people whose nervous systems are going to be dysregulated. We know that we can self-regulate and co-regulate. Is it enough to solely look at teams and departments? If the sum is greater than the whole how the whole organization operates and integrates matters. **How might we better integrate?**

Structures: disintegration or reintegration

In *The Human Side of Enterprise*, written over 60 years ago, Douglas MacArthur wrote: 'The conception of an organization plan as a series of pre-determined "slots" into which individuals are selectively placed denies the whole idea of integration.'[8]

MacArthur developed 2 theories of human behaviour at work, X and Y.

Theory X assumes things like people are not intrinsically interested in work, need to be closely supervised, directed and dictated to, resist change and disklike responsibilities. Sound familiar?

Theory Y, on the other hand, suggests that when people can exercise autonomy, they are more motivated to perform at their best, be creative and seek out responsibility. If they find their job fulfilling and rewarding, they are more likely to remain loyal and committed to the organization.

MacArthur recognized that: 'Management cannot provide a man with self-respect, or with the respect of his fellows, or with the satisfaction of needs for self-fulfilment'.[9]

New theories and ways of working have emerged since that time. And yet levels of disengagement seem to suggest that Theory X is still widely practiced. Command and control type workplaces never did anything for me. How about for you?

Ana Bernardes designs learning journeys to support human workplaces. She says that when structures that have given us a form of orientation are replaced with new ways of working it can be disorientating. If the organization tries a new way of working where everyone has more freedom to make decisions but there is a lack of clarity about how to do things, people will feel lost. The organization might well revert to the previous way of working as they know it 'works'.

Ana herself joined a company that had implemented their own version of Holacracy, a self-management system. After being there for a while she noticed that the CEO still made all the decisions. She said this was acceptable as long as it was acknowledged, and everyone understood their level of decision-making.

But 'when we don't acknowledge that, it just creates insecurity in us because we are told that we have the authority and the responsibility, but then we don't feel like it'.

As a result, everyone becomes unsure of where they stand or how to address it. This instils a sense of instability and fear amongst people even if they can't work out where it comes from because on some level they agreed to this new structure.

Ana cautions that: 'just because we have the right software and we have a diagram of how things should work, this doesn't mean that people are ready to perceive the workplace in a different way'. To be able to engage with new ways of working, people need to be more self-aware and communicate more effectively and think outside the structure(d) box.[10]

Design for one or for many?

Until recently, I thought the word trauma was reserved for huge life-changing events, like a natural disaster or terrorism. While studying Social Impact Strategy at the University of Pennsylvania my understanding of trauma, amongst many other things, changed. Dr Gabor Maté describes trauma as something that happens inside of us as a result of what happened to us.[11]

Kaveh Sadeghian, Creative Director and Founding Member of the University of Pennsylvania's Center for Social Impact Strategy, told me that there were many different definitions of trauma, and he categorizes it as something that we don't have the space to process, so it becomes internalized. Kaveh distinguished between trauma with a capital T and with a lowercase t.

'T' trauma describes catastrophic events like earth-quakes and acts of terrorism. Whereas, 't' trauma describes events like being chastised at school for being 'bad' at maths, being picked on at school or at home, a break-up, being fired or made redundant. Our reaction to any of these events is individual and can exponentially differ to another's. **Your experience is your experience, and as your experience it is absolutely valid.**

There isn't necessarily a sliding scale of traumatic events, despite the T/t distinction here. We can all carry traumas around with us and they become part of our past experiences that impact our predictions and future actions.

Kaveh talked about the importance of acknowledging the fact that organizations are living and breathing entities with their own cultures that can, in and of themselves, experience and perpetuate trauma. If you think of someone that might be experiencing post-traumatic stress disorder (PTSD) who becomes hypervigilant and hypersensitive you can also see that manifest at an organizational level. People may be incredibly nervous that they might say the wrong thing, make mistakes or they don't feel comfortable raising issues or reporting them.

The pace of trust

When we try to solve these workplace issues Kaveh thinks we tend to jump to *the many* with our solutions. We try to design systems that we can scale and Kaveh believes this is where we lose people, lose trust and belonging. As he says even the word *system* is such a non-empathetic word. Instead, we might get further by asking how we design systems that are compassionate.

'Compassionate... the word literally means to feel the suffering of another. To feel. And it starts with that. We have to learn how to interrogate and acknowledge our biases towards moving to systems and scale immediately, and then acknowledge that a lot of these interventions have to be created slowly over time.

Your solutions will move at the pace of trust.

And that starts with individuals talking to each other, listening to each other, repeating back what they've heard and making sure they got it right. And then from pairs into small groups.'[12]

How might we create environments where people can thrive? In recent years Simon Sinek got many of us thinking about 'our why'. The pandemic catapulted wellbeing at work front and centre on our agenda. Are solutions being designed for the many, scaled and systematized, without fully understanding that the foundation, the basics, the environment is already on shaky ground?

Kaveh says we have to acknowledge the why, the what, the who and the how we work together. In a world where there are lots of team and accountability structures and where performance is constantly being measured there is a feeling that we need to act, behave or produce in a certain way.

How might we create cultures and spaces where people are actively given permission to show up as themselves, to showcase their passions, values and know that their work is going to respect those values?

We are living in a hybrid world

At the time of writing, there is an ongoing debate as to what the future of work(places) will look like. Some leaders want everyone back in the office. Others no longer have an office. When we first went into lock-down I was no stranger to the world of remote work. In my last role, 10 out of 12 colleagues, who reported to me, lived and worked in different countries to me. Technology enables us to do so much and has fundamentally changed the traditional ways of working. It has given us options and flexibility.

Can you change how you feel about your work whether you are working remotely or in the office?

If the culture of the organization is not conducive to doing your best work that is what needs to be addressed. With everyone working remotely it can mask the issue, but the cracks will begin to show. I don't think the answer is forcing everyone back into the office either. It will never revert to the way it was before. People want flexibility, autonomy to choose. And that might look different within and between organizations.

I believe there is something about using video technology that levels the playing field. On the screen we are all the same size. Perhaps it alters power dynamics and interpersonal dynamics? We have a window into people's lives, outside the office, that we didn't always have. However, if ineffective communication was an issue prior to leaving the office I doubt it has been solved simply by changing the channel. We still need to know how to communicate effectively to perform optimally. Investing in better technology isn't always the answer. **We need to understand the value of humans interacting together and the dividends we will reap from in-person interpersonal creativity and collaboration.**

In *Wired for Love*, neuroscientist Stephanie Cacioppo, PhD, says that our social connections 'have not only shaped the human brain throughout its evolution; they also continue to shape the brain throughout the course of an individual human's life'. What our brain 'benefits from, what it *needs*, is a rich reciprocal connection with someone else, or something else. It doesn't matter how many connections you have or how society expects them to look; what matters, ultimately, for your physical as well as psychological wellbeing is the quality of those social connections'.[13]

I firmly believe that there are times when we need to be in a room together, we need the energy of others to create and make progress. We need to share meals and laughter together. **We need to get a feel for, or the measure of, one another.**

John Fairhurst is Head of Private Sector Engagement at the Global Fund and we talked about the importance of knowing what the right way of working really looks like. John says organizations need to make an investment in what makes organizations thrive, and to understand how people work together and engage effectively. On the one hand the ability to be able to work from different places and to engage in the workplace in a completely different way has created an incredibly positive environment and flexibility which is valued by and valuable to people. But on the other hand, it has created an environment of back-to-back meetings where even your commute time has become about getting work done, which is also part of the flexibility. John says:

> 'For me, a lot of the energy around the workplace is about people and being able to engage with and have conversations that are not directly work related. In a remote work setting, it's much harder to have that interpersonal engagement and to do things around collaboration and to work on innovation. I think it is so much harder than in a video call context.
>
> For new people coming into the organization, it's harder to get integrated, it's harder to create career progression. And there's lots of evidence that it's also harder for women as well. I'm not sure the solution is to make everyone come back to the office 5 days a week either, which is what some organizations are doing. I think there's so much in the current way of working that is better than the traditional 5 days a week in the office.'

John said that if organizations want to be successful, they need take the impact of the news being full of unprecedented heat waves, natural disasters and conflict on people into account. Given that we spend the vast majority of our life working we need to look after ourselves and whether organizations like it or not, we're working in that global context and therefore this translates into *how we feel at work*.[14]

Human skills speaker, Nick Jemetta, says wellbeing is a complex, multifaceted issue that needs to be prioritized and needs time and investment. Creating a checklist is not good enough as it doesn't demonstrate the right intention. Nick would rather see people in organizations doing less to support others as long as they are doing it with the right intention. According to Nick mental health and wellbeing should pervade every aspect of the organization because 'fundamentally, it's just about people'. Nick says:

> 'People have a life. Work is one facet of that, but when they come to work, every other facet is coming with them. Encourage that. Let them bring all of those things to work. Be open about it and support them as and when they need that.'

You do need to speak to people to find out if they feel supported. Nick says we need to treat people fairly and recognize them for who they are and although wellbeing has become 'this complex, slightly mysterious topic', it doesn't need to be.[15]

Remember Sam's and Alex's charts in Chapter 7. We might never know how our colleagues really feel.

Or are we living in a VUCA world?

VUCA is an acronym often used to describe the world that we are living and working in. **VUCA stands for volatility, uncertainty, complexity and ambiguity.**

If we just think of this in terms of people and our moods, feelings, emotions and nervous systems. When it comes to people interacting with one another it isn't always straight-forward. We are all doing our best to make our way in the world and it is important that our relationships are interactional and not transactional. People cannot be accounted for in the same way that money is. There can't be a *one-size fits all* approach to people. **You never really know what is going on inside someone else and even someone who appears outwardly calm can feel volatile inside.**

What are the skills we need to embrace to do our best in this world?

I came up with an *alternative* VUCA: vulnerable, under-standing, caring and authentic.

- **Vulnerable:** Vulnerability is a strength; it takes courage to be vulnerable in front of others and it builds connection.
- **Understanding:** We need people who are willing to listen to us to understand us. We all want to be understood and accepted for who we are and what we bring to the world.
- **Caring:** President Roosevelt said that 'No one cares how much you know until they know how much you care'.
- **Authentic:** And we need to be authentic – we need to mean what we say and act accordingly.

Personally, I prefer the word genuine, but it didn't quite work. I can be flexible.

When all is said and done, I believe Maya Angelou said it best: 'I've learned that people will forget what you said, people will forget what you did, but people will never forget how you made them feel'.

Strengthening social intelligence

Social skills are often overlooked, under-appreciated and undervalued. Why is there a lack of engagement at work? Because people are overlooked, under-appreciated and undervalued.

Have we been going about this all wrong? So-called *soft skills* are not soft. They take courage. They take strength. They take inner work. Developing social intelligence can accelerate your growth in the world. If your inner world is more at peace, you can face the outer world with presence and poise. At work you will clearly see that how you feel about your work, how you feel at work and the feelings of all those around you impact the bottom line.

If social skills impact the bottom line let's draw attention to them. Let's talk about them in a way that makes business sense. Let's use the language of business to bring home the importance of social intelligence, the value added of embracing the intangible as well as the tangible. And let's bring it back to basics.

- How does your brain work?
- How does your body work?
- How do they work together?

- What do I need to be my best self at work and at life?
- What do I need to be comfortable facing situations I'd rather avoid?

- What do I need to do to be able to accept responsibility for my inner world?

- How do I work in relationship to others?
- How can I see the best in people, their humanity?
- What do I need to do to treat others fairly, respect-
  fully and best?

A focus on inner growth and development is needed. It does take work. And there are people all around the world doing this work. You don't have to go it alone, as an organization or individually. There is support available and one initiative in particular I believe is worth drawing your attention to is the inner development goals (IDGs).

Inner development goals

The sustainable development goals (SDGs), launched by the United Nations in 2015, set out a plan, of 17 broad and comprehensive goals to be reached by 2030, to secure a sustainable future for people and planet. The SDGs are a vision for a sustainable future. People are committed to fulfilling this vision and there is large-scale funding available for these efforts. Nonetheless progress has been slow.

Why? People began to ask that very question. And why crises appeared to be getting bigger, more complex and daunting. Was there a missing ingredient or a blind spot?

Academics, business leaders, psychologists and thought leaders all reached similar conclusions – a critical element was missing.

Our efforts to resolve or even put a dent in some of the crises the world faces are both supported and undermined by human behaviour. As humans we find it difficult to work together and not all of us have developed the inner capacity to deal effectively with increasingly complex challenges in an inter-connected world. Despite making phenomenal advances in the (outer) world we have to an extent ignored the development of our inner world, perhaps even discon- necting ourselves further from it. **A thriving inner world influences our capacity to thrive in the outer world which will help the planet thrive.**

Following a consultation process a team of international researchers produced the IDGs framework. The IDGs frame- work is made up of 5 categories, outlined below, that include 23 skills and qualities for human inner growth and develop- ment. IDGs is a not-for-profit and open-source initiative for you to use.[16]

Being	Relationship to self
Thinking	Cognitive skills
Relating	Caring for others and the world
Collaborating	Social skills
Acting	Enabling change

Katharina Moser, a member of the Executive Board of the IDGs, told me that many of us have 'this innate feeling that something is not quite right, and we should change some- thing'. It can be difficult for individuals to initiate changes on their own. Often certain life events are the catalyst for people to begin their own inner work. Katharina says we shouldn't wait for a tragedy to understand the power of inner development. Inner development can affect all aspects of your life and have a ripple effect.

She gave an example of Tomas Björkman, a successful Swedish businessman and founder of the Ekskäret Foundation, which is one of the initial institutions that founded the IDGs. He brought consultants into his organization to do leadership trainings. Working with them he realized that inner work had a positive impact on him, his life and on his organization.

Katharina highlights the importance of the IDGs in promoting the idea that individuals do not need to do this work alone. Rather it can be done '... as a collective. And we do it in order to change our culture so that we have inner development as a crucial part of our society and of who we are as human beings. And out of that a completely different world can emerge'. We can make inner work a normal part of our life's work and work-life.

She also says that inner work is not anything new. Inner development has been something people have done for a long time, in different ways. What the IDGs do is draw on ancient wisdom traditions, leadership trainings, coaching and consulting institutions to bring together individuals with a similar vision and create a common language and framework. She believes that this collective effort will connect many people and lead to a ripple of change.[17]

The bottom line: A thriving culture relies on all people attuning to their inner world.

9

Why doesn't everyone just get along – who is accountable and who is responsible?

'Work is love made visible.'

Khalil Gibran

A snapshot: Once we understand ourselves better, we can better understand others.

Our common humanity

The father of accounting may have been inspired by the merchants of Venice. As a 14-year-old I was inspired by Shakespeare's *The Merchant of Venice* and in particular by these words:

> 'I am a Jew. Hath not a Jew eyes? Hath not a Jew hands, organs, dimensions, senses, affections, passions? Fed with the same food, hurt with the same weapons, subject to the same diseases, healed by the same

means, warmed and cooled by the same winter and summer as a Christian is? If you prick us, do we not bleed? If you tickle us, do we not laugh? If you poison us, do we not die? And if you wrong us, shall we not revenge?'

About the same time, I was studying Shylock, I remember seeing an essay title on an English state exam paper that students were asked to discuss *Man's Inhumanity to Man*. Although I didn't have to answer that I remember being struck by the statement. I still wonder why we are inhumane towards one another. Is it time to focus on man's *humanity* to man? On our common humanity?

We are all human beings. We are also all different and unique. We think differently, work differently, process differently, see differently, love differently and live differently. If we work from the premise that people are just people first and foremost, and different from me is okay, is it possible to make the world of work a more tolerable and hospitable place? Is it possible that this will increase levels of engagement?

Imagine a workplace where every single individual at work regardless of their level of qualifications, their background, their technical skills and abilities was totally comfortable in their own skin. If everyone was attuned to their inner world they would tune into the world of others in more constructive and collaborative ways. Improving bodily and emotional intelligence enables us to become more socially intelligent. Our cognitive intelligence is crucial but oftentimes it can be our blind spot and we can idealize it to the point of ignoring all the other intelligence we hold. We need them all.

It is the responsibility of every single person to treat every other human, whether they are their colleague, teammate, boss, director or customer, with dignity. Technical skills only get us so far. Social skills take us much further. It is way too easy to dismiss people management as something that is the responsibility of human resources (HR) or to delegate your responsibilities to HR. Just because we are all people, we cannot assume that we will get on with all people or that all people know how to relate to, communicate and collaborate with others.

It's not you, it's me

There might be more to this pithy comment than we dare to admit. From a young age we condition ourselves to hide from being blamed or taking responsibility for our mistakes in the hope that someone else will. Some of us get really proficient at it and find ourselves in leadership positions. Others shrink in their shadow each day affirming their perceived lack of worth as if the world is, most definitely, stacked against them.

But it's not them or you, it is me. And once I understand that, feel it deeply I can start to think differently – in a way that changes this. We are the sum total of our experiences. And as we have seen our experiences help us to efficiently, albeit not always optimally, respond to the context we are in.

My experiences are meaningful to me precisely because they are meaningful to me. They might not even register for you; they may be completely meaningless. But that is ok as it's not you, it's me. I suspect this serves to reinforce silos and separation in workplaces. For example, if you approach someone in finance with a request, the lens at which they look at your question through might be a risk lens or a cost control lens or even a 'just say no' lens. Those lenses are meaningful to them because of their training, background and experience. Their neural pathways are well worn. And the response may well be a default one.

The antidote? Curiosity.

See the person, not their response or their behaviour. Try to understand from their perspective, their lens why their prescribed course of action is meaningful to them. And do the same for yourself – understand why you avoid a certain person or process yet willingly engage with others. We need to understand ourselves more. And once more of us understand that we will feel a responsibility to create the conditions that encourage and facilitate others to do the same. **Once we understand ourselves better, we can better understand others.**

Although you're not ultimately responsible for anyone else's feelings other than your own, until you take responsibility for your feelings you will definitely impact others. This isn't about walking on eggshells but walking more consciously and collaboratively. Not everyone wishes us well. Not everyone has our best interest or even anyone's interest at heart. And then it is them, not you. It isn't your job to fix them, change them, appease them. **You are responsible for you.**

Understanding your own internal sensations can change your perception and experiences. In uncertainty, you can navigate feelings that arise and distinguish between discomfort and distress, feeling unsafe, or suffering. Once you take responsibility, you'll also be accountable, own up, take the blame and accept the praise. You'll be comfortable being uncomfortable. All of this is made possible when we account for our emotions.

Why doesn't everyone just get along?

In a workplace people are present to work towards a shared goal, strategy, mission or vision. It shouldn't really matter what your role is, who your boss is or how many are in your department. What matters is your attitude towards, and ability to work with, others to achieve a result. It sounds simple. Doesn't it?

This isn't some wild, crazy, unfathomable idea or ideal. It isn't a utopian dream that grown-ups, adults or humans can work alongside each other to achieve a result. We need to be in alignment.

Yet the current workplaces of the world aren't the most conducive to collaborative endeavours. What does it mean to collaborate and are there conditions conducive to collaboration? To collaborate means to work with at least one other individual to achieve a shared outcome.

Collaboration differs from consensus. When we reach a consensus, we have general agreement. It doesn't necessarily mean that everyone agrees but everyone needs to be able to accept the course of action, willingly.

At times collaboration requires compromise. Compromising might require making concessions – we might have to relent on something we wanted in service of the whole.

True collaboration means people involved get their say, are heard, and their suggestions or approaches are discussed, deconstructed, reconstructed, accepted or dismissed.

Can you recall a successful collaboration at work? What made it successful?

One reason collaboration can be difficult is when people don't really care about the outcome. They are no longer engaged; they've checked out and are merely going through the (e)motions. When people feel it isn't worth the effort, it doesn't matter, their opinion doesn't count, no one listens when they speak – they are less inclined to. Sam or Alex, for example, might think to themselves 'Isn't it best to just keep my head down, agree with whatever so I can just get back to my desk or get out of here?'.

Hierarchy or authority, perceived or real, can be a challenge to collaboration. People might not feel confident to say what they genuinely think when they are asked to contribute. They might not feel confident making suggestions, or think their idea is so simple, so basic, that it must have thought of it before. A group leader can set the tone and the tone may intimate 'my way or the highway'. This leaves no room for challenge or discussion. This is coercion, compliance or conformity, not collaboration. And the more they defend their stance, the *right* stance, the less they listen to anyone else's *right* stance. They listen to respond, and defend, not to understand.

I don't want to talk about it

This leads nicely into another reason collaboration can be difficult. Conflict. When we begin to defend our stance, it can become personal. Perhaps our idea or approach is tried and tested and so we dig our heels in and begin to cut people off as they raise objections or ignore what other people say entirely or begin an internal dialogue while ignoring everything else that is being said. For example:

How dare they?

Typical bloody response from Sam – it is always the same thing over and over like a broken record.

Alex is so self-absorbed and just loves to talk and most of it is just repeating what others have said but with fancier language.

I can't believe they can't see that my suggestion is the best way forward. We'll never get out of here at this rate.

It might not result in full-blown conflict; we might not raise our voices or get angry with one another as we prefer to avoid conflict. We simply stew. Or some voices get raised and others go quiet. The situation unravels and remains unresolved. Until the next day when we get back together again and go through the whole thing once more. And again, the next day. Eventually someone gets worn down or we come up with some half-baked compromise as we all just want to move on.

When we go home that evening and are recounting the day, we say it was another disaster. And despair at how it is such a shame that nobody knows what they are doing and at this rate we are never going to get anywhere, and it isn't a surprise really as if they'd only done what we said, and knew, worked then we would actually get the result we were after.

As all of us are working towards a common goal, strategy, mission or vision.

There are multiple factors at play that challenge collaboration. In an ideal world it would be so much easier if everyone we worked with was on our wavelength. Then everyone would know where they stood, and we could just get on with it.

And pigs will fly over the blue moon. Of course, if we were all robots then that would solve the problem. Would it? A robot will do what you tell it to do or programme it to do. It will do its own individual task or part. It isn't going to go to a meeting or a workshop and collaborate with you. Yet.

We need the capacity to disagree with one another, to push one another, to push back, to agree not because we feel we have no option but because we believe there is a better option. We need diverse voices and contributions too. We've evolved as a species because of our ability to collaborate. The tag line of *The Evolving Leaders'* podcast sums this up nicely **'The world is evolving, are you?'**

Are you?

It's the relationships that counts

Douglas MacArthur said leadership is 'a relationship with different situations'. I like this.

I often think that leadership is the ability to say I don't know. Being a leader certainly requires a relationship with uncertainty. To be comfortable with uncertainty requires a secure relationship with yourself. We can learn a lot about ourselves through our relationships with others and with different situations but our relationship to self is a key building block.

Do you know who you are when no one else is around?

'It was all about the people' is a phrase I've heard in so many leaving speeches, in conversations and, I've said it myself. We are social beings. Working in relation to one another requires being in a relationship. It almost goes without saying that healthy working relationships are critical to creating an environment conducive to collaboration, creativity and change.

The Happiness Index consistently finds that the quality of relationships between colleagues has the greatest influence on employee happiness. Feedback, interestingly, is next on the list.[1] Giving and receiving feedback has a lot to do with how we relate to and communicate with one another.

Do you know how the people you work with would describe your relationship? How do you relate to one another? Who are you in relation to them?

Healthy high performance

Sheila Walsh joined Car Trawler as Director of People and within 2.5 years became Chief People Officer (CPO). Prior to being appointed CPO, she worked hard to help build its people-centric culture. The organization was team-player based and for her it was quite unique in that regard. She said that the Leadership Team work hard to cultivate and maintain this.

'There is such a collegiate atmosphere. We don't
nurture rockstars or Mavericks or big egos. And I've
worked for so long in so many different companies,
it's so rare. It's fantastic. We're so lucky to be together.
It's like alchemy when it all comes together... it's
nearly like pixie dust.'

The Leadership Team works with a team coach who Sheila
says, 'whips us into shape every couple of months and keeps
tabs on us'. This coach does not let them get comfortable or
complacent and helps them to 'ruthlessly prioritize' and to
maintain peer-to-peer accountability whilst being focused
on the results. The benefit of this, Sheila believes, is like it
is for any sports team because they don't wait 6 months or
longer to revisit anything that needs to be addressed. Sheila
said that the bar is constantly being set which is challenging,
but in a good way. She was appreciative of being able to work
with a team coach and of having that investment in the leadership team. She believed it made them a better team.

The team adhere to Patrick Lencioni's *Five Dysfunctions
of a Team* model. They focus on the core fundamentals of
organizational clarity, communicating that clarity, over
communicating that clarity and minimizing confusion and
politics. Sheila said, 'when that's present then you have the
good stuff'. For Sheila 'the good stuff' is that you're creating
the conditions for people to flourish and thrive. Sheila said
the Leadership Team strive to ensure they are role modelling
'the good stuff'. Although they might fall short at times, they
have each other's backs and can acknowledge when someone

has had a rough week or needs some extra support. They *get* that rough weeks are part of being human.

The Leadership Team realized that they didn't want to have a high-performing culture at the cost of people's health. They inserted the word healthy into their organizational strategy to strive for *healthy, high performance*. They focused on cascading, what they call, organizational health – practical guidance on things like how to run good meetings, how to prioritize, how to focus on the strategy. Sheila believes that healthy, high performance has cascaded throughout the organization and that anyone would say they love their teammates, what they are working on and how they work together.[2]

Emotional data

The Happiness Index is a modern version of an employee engagement platform. Co-founder, Matt Phelan, told me that they combine instinctive and emotional data on how people feel with rational and reflective data on how people think.

Matt says that most employee engagement technology has focused on the rational part of what an employee experience is. Matt says this part is important but only one part of the story. The Happiness Index is built on neuroscience, and they go further to provide a better understanding. Matt says that instead of saying 'if you can measure it, you can manage it', he now says 'if you can measure it, you can better understand it. If you can better understand it, you can make better decisions. You still might get decisions wrong, but you are more informed in your decision making. Data is about improving your decision making.'

When I asked him to explain the 4 dimensions, he used the following example. Imagine Peter who is about to be interviewed to be an HR manager:

1. We have our first impression – our instinctive response to that person. We can't control an instinctive response.
2. If Peter happens to look like your ex-husband, your brother, your worst enemy, your best friend or like Tom Jones you will have an emotional response. This is the second dimension.
3. Third is a rational response. He's done 5 years in a similar role and has the required qualifications.
4. Our fourth dimension is our reflective response.

Instinctively you had a good first impression. You get over the fact that they look like your ex-husband quickly because your rational thinking kicks in and they've got a good CV. And you just wait until tomorrow to decide. You reflect on it.

He says as humans we like to simplify stuff, but life doesn't work like that. While your gut is important, and you should listen to your gut you should not let it solely make life's big decisions for you. You should question where your data is coming from. Is there enough data in your experience? Is the data biased? Our personal database is driven by our experiences and the only thing you can do to improve this database is gain new and varied experiences. Most biases have evolved to protect us, and your body is giving you instinctive data, for example, we all have a bias to not eat poisonous food which could be argued to be a good thing. However, it is important to be aware that if we want to move from survival mode to thrive mode that we need to understand our biases and move them from being unconscious to conscious. Our biases can result in us making terrible decisions in work and life, so it is important to work hard to better understand them.

When making important decisions don't ignore your gut but do try and blend in some emotional, rational and reflective data sources.[3]

I'm biased

There are numerous biases to be aware, and beware, of. One bias I find a helpful one to remind myself of is what is known as fundamental attribution error (FAE).

I'll use an everyday example to illustrate. Alex sent an email to a number of people and asked them all to reply to Alex only. Sam hits reply-all when replying. Alex immediately jumps to the conclusion that Sam did this intentionally and was always out to embarrass Alex. A couple of days later Alex hits reply-all when asked not to. When Alex realizes what they did they shrug it off as just one of those things that happens when you are trying to do too many things at once.

We tend to overlook the possibility that someone else's behaviour was a consequence of their context but are able to justify our own behaviour as we know our own context. Be open to possibilities and alternative explanations.

If it starts with you, how do you get started?

Great question. Right.

Perhaps start by selecting the one thing that struck you most while reading through this book. The thing that stirred something inside of you. That was data to pay attention to. If you were struck by several things, then start with the one that you are most curious about and go deeper.

If none of them sufficiently piqued your curiosity, you might consider experimenting with this one that I found in the book *Presence*. It relates to seeing yourself, or *presence-ing* yourself, in your organizational culture through observation and reflective participation. People actively participate in a culture and keep it alive. We embody the culture even if we would rather not.

The authors suggest to continue to participate as normal in typical meetings and 'learn to pay attention to the "external" dynamics of the meeting as well as to your own thoughts and feelings'. After the meeting, set aside some time to reflect on an incident where you were emotionally engaged. Re-create what you were thinking and feeling as the incident played out. You can recruit your imagination to help with this. It might be valuable for you to write your experiences down or talk them through with a colleague.

You can learn about yourself and your organization if you intentionally repeat this process several times. 'You'll see where you felt safe and where you felt threatened. You'll see where you were conflicted and where you were aligned with what was happening around you. You'll see where you were distracted and where you were fully present. As you practice this, you'll be able to engage your imagination more actively to "see" the details of your experience.'

Next you can begin to imagine the incident through the perspective of one or more of your colleagues. Reflect on the similarities and differences. 'While your experience in shifting your point of view appears to tell you about the experiences of others, what you're really doing is using your imagination to explore further subtleties of your own experience. Unless they tell you, you have no way of knowing what others actually experience. But you will discover what you were experiencing about others and, empathetically, how the organization's norms and habits are manifested in different people.'

Once you see how the culture lives in people and you are a part of the culture, if you ask: "'What am I doing – in my actions, thoughts and feelings – to maintain these patterns as they are?" you will see many ways that you play a part and perhaps a few new options for what you might do differently.'[4]

In *Nine Lies About Work*, Marcus Buckingham and Ashley Goodall recommend that rather than striving for balance between work and life to find love in what you do. They highlight that the Mayo Clinic measured the power of love in work at found that physicians who spend at least 20% of their time doing things they loved had a significantly lower risk of burning out. They recommend playing to your strengths as a way to weave love intentionally and responsibly into your work because *love-in-work matters most*, not work–life balance.[5]

Explore your creativity

We are all creative and if you aren't conscious of your creative spark, it is in there somewhere waiting to be enticed out into the world. You will inspire yourself when you connect with your creativity. We can be creative in a variety of ways – through writing, art, music, dance, movement, comedy, gardening, cookery and more. Do you know what makes your heart sing?

And we can encourage our creativity at work. By thinking creatively, we can reimagine and recreate the workplaces of the future.

The bottom line: Our interactions, interconnectedness and relationships help us better understand who we are.

The bottom line: It's more than a feeling

'Yesterday I was clever, so I wanted to change the world. Today I am wise, so I am changing myself.'

Rumi

Your future self

'Every day is a possibility to discover a new story.'[1] I heard this line while listening to a podcast, and it is one I remind myself of regularly. Every day we have an opportunity to discover a new story or reframe an old story. This means that every day brings possibility to account for our lives in a different way or to rebalance an imbalance. The basics will always be the same and the more we know about what our basics the more we can be the accountant, or author, of our story.

When we set out to explore and generate alternatives, they exist. The key is to begin the exploration. The conductor Benjamin Zander realized in his 40s that the conductor of an orchestra doesn't make a sound. Instead, his power depends on his ability to make other people powerful. In *The Art of Possibility*, we are reminded that everything in the world is invented and when everything is invented the world is full of possibilities. We should stand in possibility and awaken possibilities in others. Oh, and to abide by rule no. 6 – not to take yourself too seriously.[2]

We already saw that combining conceptual and embodied self-awareness can be a powerful fuel for growth. In an Oscar acceptance speech, Matthew McConaghy spoke about 3 things that he needs every day – something to look up to, something to look forward to and someone to chase. He chases his hero, his future self, who he will be in 10 years. He says he will never attain that, but he is ok with that because he always has someone to chase.[3]

When people feel that their work has no meaning, that they aren't contributing to something greater than themselves, that they don't have the opportunity to use their unique strengths and talents, that they aren't being seen or heard or valued it has a ripple effect on colleagues, customers, suppliers and then on to family, friends, community, society, nature and the world. Find possibility. Find meaning. Find someone to chase.

To capture the essence of what I hope you take away from this book I created an acronym from the image of the SEESAW. The seesaw image on the book cover is a visual reminder of the complexities of balance.

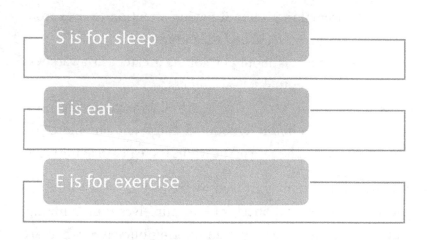

S is for sleep

E is eat

E is for exercise

- **Sleep** is vital to our health and wellbeing. Build a solid sleep habit. It is foundational.
- **Eating** what is optimal for you and staying hydrated helps your body-budgeting help you.
- **Exercise** has plenty of benefits for us and remember *the best exercise is exercise you are going to do.*

Ensuring that these basic bodily needs are being proportionately met will pay dividends.

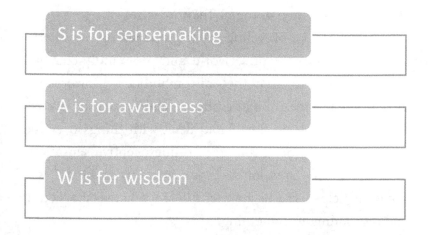

S is for sensemaking

A is for awareness

W is for wisdom

- **S**ensemaking is about paying attention to data from your inner world *and* the outer world.
- **A**wareness is about developing greater self-awareness and conceptual self-awareness.
- **W**isdom is about leveraging all of your intelligences: cognitive, bodily, emotional, social and any more you discover. The sum of the whole is greater than the parts.

Increasing our own self-awareness is a continuous journey. Taking an honest look at ourselves, our thinking, our feelings, our behaviour, and asking ourselves when are we at our best? When we don't think, feel and act at our best we can ask ourselves what our own contribution was to that. Taking an honest look at our own situation can be risky. Admitting that we are in over our heads, that we are unfulfilled, too stressed or unhappy isn't always easy. As we have seen we can normalize it and justify it to ourselves.

From my own experience it is a long way back; don't keep accruing a metabolic tax that prices you out of the market. If you do, your body or your brain, or both, will put a stop to it at some point. Listen to them. They are wise.

The simple act of feeling my feet opened up my interoceptive and proprioceptive world and profoundly changed my life. I began to strengthen my embodied self-awareness. This also led to me strengthening my conceptual self-awareness by reflecting on how I had dealt with things over the years, how I had been tuning into interoceptive sensations even if I wasn't consciously aware that this is what I was doing. It helped me to *get* the difference between reacting and responding to something.

How empowering is that?

Next steps

What are you going to do next? Before you decide. I have a couple of questions for you.

Are you appropriately selfish?

Jerry Harris has a portfolio non-executive director career. When I asked him about work–life balance he reflected on how much organizations have changed throughout his career. He said he didn't remember when he heard people speak about work–life balance first but told me that one of his bosses spoke to him about 'appropriate selfishness':

> 'It's an interesting phrase. It doesn't sound that good, but there is an element of that phrase that says that there are certain things that are important to you that you need to do, to operate in a good way. You need to know what they are and make sure you get enough of them. And if that doesn't work with other people, be it in your work or your home or other things, then something's got to change. Because if you're not getting enough of the things you need in the right way, then that, sooner or later, unravels.'[4]

Do you know where your boundaries are? I've always found that most people respect them when they know where they are.

Who has your back?

In *Influence is Your Superpower,* Zoe Chance points out that we've been taught to be self-sufficient and generous. This can deplete us. We will offer to help people before they ask or agree to lend a hand when asked. Yet we don't always seek support ourselves. We believe we can go it alone, manage ourselves, and get on with it.[5]

We have a saying in Ireland '*Ar scáth a chéile a mhaireann na daoine*' which translates as we live in one another's shadows, but means we depend on each other not only to survive but to thrive, that we shelter one another and have each other's backs.

Does someone have your back?

Small steps

There are lots of different techniques in this book to explore. Taking small steps can make changes seem less daunting. Putting pressure on yourself to take big steps can activate the fight or flight response and dysregulate your nervous system. Even simply slowing down can be a cue of danger to a nervous system that is always on. Small steps and daily actions are the key to changing habits.

I love to watch a sunrise and sunset. I often take photos but mostly just love to be there and be captivated by the beauty and think to myself if I had come out earlier or later, I might have missed this awesome moment. One evening I looked at some photos I had taken just 3 minutes apart. Three minutes is all it took for the sky to completely transform. Three minutes can make a massive difference. Can you find 3 minutes in your day to practice a new habit?

Maybe someone would benefit from 3 minutes of your time. If you are unable to find 3 minutes – what about 6 seconds? A study at the University of Rochester Medical Centre showed that doctors typically interrupt their patients within 23 seconds of them describing their symptoms with their diagnosis. And they also found that if the doctors had waited just 6 more seconds, the patient would have had the opportunity to share all their concerns.[6]

Can you break your next step down into smaller steps?

First steps

Learning new skills, or skills improvement, can be daunting. Humbling, even. It can involve unlearning too. In 2001, I learned to swim properly. I had been 'swimming' since I was a child, but I never learned how to breathe properly and synchronize the strokes with my breath. Relearning was costly, but wise, as I had to replace old habits with new ones. I remember the words of the swim teacher clearly: 'take one thing at a time because if you try to change everything at once you will forget to breathe'. She was right.

What is your first step? When will you take it?

For your onward journey some inspiring words from the Spanish poet Antonio Machado: **'Traveller there is no path, the path is made by walking.'**

Before you go

Our journey together has almost ended. Here are a few final reminders.

Variation is the norm. Embrace it.

We all have a *voice*. It is what we do with it that counts. Tune into the *Life Beyond the Numbers* podcast if you want to hear mine.

What we feel on the inside can differ from what is *visible* to the outside world. What the outside world perceives can also vary.

We can all be unhappy, dissatisfied, discontent and find fault. And worry about all the things that we could have done better or differently. Reflection is important. The ability to take an honest look at ourselves, our choices, our fears, hopes and desires. We *can* do this alone. I have found that getting it out of my head makes a difference. We can do this by writing. Having another human bear witness to our thoughts and feelings is powerful too. And that doesn't have to be through our words alone, it can be through sound, art or movement and probably in other ways too.

You can spend your life avoiding things that feel uncomfortable and feel difficult for you or you can accept that these feelings are part of being human and you can move through the world with greater ease by tuning into, and being more aware of, your brain and your body, your thoughts and feelings. You can show up for the other human and focus on being compassionate towards them. That is an honourable intention. Our presence is the best gift we can give anyone. Being there for another human can have a profound impact.

Emotions tip the balance

Emotions guide what we do at work. By dismissing the most unique element of what makes us human as noise or interference we have failed to generate the best behaviours to enable better collaboration, creativity, decisions, performance, relationships, results and workplaces. Connecting mind and body and embedding a 'both–and' approach pays dividends. We are all shaped by our experiences, but we have the ability to reshape ourselves and our futures. Investing in elevating the role of our inner world and emotions will increase revenue and retention and decrease conflict, disengagement and mistrust.

Don't be a number. Numbers don't make decisions, numbers don't do the work, numbers don't feel, numbers can't do anything without people. So, be yourself. Be human. Be. And if you can't do that where you are, seek the place that you can – that is what I ask of you, dear reader. Don't settle for someone else's account of what life is supposed to be like, write your own story. You are the only one who is accountable. **The bottom line is that accounting for emotions tips the balance at work.**

Appendix

Key questions

Introduction

- How might we balance emotion and professionalism?
- Is it because we account for people as costs that we don't always recognize how invaluable they are?
- If it can't be measured, can we afford to ignore it?

Chapter 1

- Although we are not in physical danger (in the workplace), are we physiologically and psychologically safe?
- Can we put the blame on people who feel disengaged for being disengaged?
- Do you know what gets you out of bed each morning?

Chapter 2

- What story does the balance sheet tell?
- Does the number on your birthday tell your story?
- What are your assets, liabilities and equity?

Chapter 3

- How many of us pursue careers because we found something easy to do in school and that ability was encouraged?
- Does our expertise preclude us from considering other perspectives?
- Have you been told that you are more left- or right-brained?

Chapter 4

- Have you ever thought, my body let me down?
- Are you conscious of how you bring your presence to every conversation and interaction whether it is a one-on-one with a direct report or speaking to a room full of shareholders?
- Do you ever think about your breath or breathing? Do you notice when it quickens or slows?

Chapter 5

- Can you describe your mood?
- How many emotion words do you know?
- What makes a conversation difficult?

Chapter 6

- What did you takeaway from these stories?
- What would you have done differently in their shoes?
- What will you do differently after reading them?

Chapter 7

- Do you feel resourced to live and work as your best self?
- Why do we sleep?
- If I asked you to tell me *honestly how much stress you are under. What would you say?*

Chapter 8

- Do you know who you are without your job title?
- Does your voice count?
- How might we create environments where people can thrive?

Chapter 9

- Do you know how the people you work with would describe your relationship?
- Is there enough data in your gut?
- If it starts with you, how do you get started?

The bottom line

- What is your next step?
- Can you break that into smaller steps?
- What is your first step?

Notes

Introduction

[1] Elizabeth Lesser, *Cassandra Speaks: When Women are the Storytellers, the Human Story Changes.* (Harper Collins, 2020, p. 245)

[2] This definition is from International Financial Reporting Standards (IFRS): 'IAS 38 - Intangible Assets' www.ifrs.org/issued-standards/list-of-standards/ias-38-intangible-assets/ (last accessed 28 October, 2023)

Chapter 1: A growing (or going) concern

[1] Gallup's *State of the World Global Workplace: 2023* Report shows that 23% of employees are engaged at work. www.gallup.com/

[2] ibid.

[3] World Travel and Tourism Website https://wttc.org/Portals/0/Documents/Press%20Releases/Travel-and-Tourism-could-grow-to-8.6-trillion-USD-in-2022-says-WTTC.pdf?ver=oEtiQMTnaavQuT3K7mUhYQ%3d%3d (last accessed 24 August, 2023).

[4] The Prince's Responsible Business Network, *Prioritise People: Unlock the Value of a Thriving Workforce* prepared by Business in the Community's (BITC) Wellbeing Leadership Team with support and research from McKinsey Health Institute (MHI) (24 April, 2023). www.bitc.org.uk/report/prioritise-people-unlock-the-value-of-a-thriving-workforce/ (last accessed 24 August, 2023)

[5] McKinsey Health Institute, *Addressing Employee Burnout: Are you Solving the Right Problem?* (27 March, 2022) www.mckinsey.

com/mhi/our-insights/addressing-employee-burnout-are-you-solving-the-right-problem (last accessed 24 August, 2023)

[6] ReWAGE Policy Brief, *The Cost of Conflict at Work and its Impact on Productivity* https://warwick.ac.uk/fac/soc/ier/rewage/news-archive/cost_of_conflict_pb_formatted_final_2.pdf (last accessed 24 August, 2023)

[7] *Muking Numbers Count: The Art and Science of Communicating Numbers* by Chip Heath and Karla Starr. (Bantam Press, 2022, p. ix)

[8] Glin Bayley episode 39 Life Beyond the Numbers, *H.E.A.R.T.* Glin mentioned in the conversation that she heard someone say this somewhere.

[9] The Financial Conduct Authority decision notices for Carillion. www.fca.org.uk/news/press-releases/fca-publishes-decision-notices-carillion-plc-liquidation-and-three-its-former-executive-directors (last accessed 16 October, 2023)

[10] The Senior Fraud office decision for Patisserie Valerie. www.sfo.gov.uk/2023/09/13/sfo-charges-four-individuals-behind-patisserie-valerie-collapse/ (last accessed 16 October, 2023)

[11] Financial Reporting Council reports on the auditors of Carillion and Patisserie Valerie are available to read. www.frc.org.uk/news-and-events/news/2023/10/sanctions-against-kpmg-llp-kpmg-audit-plc-and-two-former-partners/ and here www.frc.org.uk/news-and-events/news/2021/09/sanctions-against-grant-thornton-uk-llp-and-david-newstead/ (last accessed 16 October, 2023)

[12] I first came across this wonderful phrase while researching for a podcast conversation with John Shinnick. You can hear more about this on episode 42, Life Beyond the Numbers, *Metamorphosis.*

13 This short, lively video covers 'autonomy, mastery and purpose'. RSA ANIMATE, *Drive: The Surprising Truth About What Motivates Us.* 1 April, 2010. www.youtube.com/watch?v=u6XAPnuFjJc

Chapter 2: Back to basics

1 Jane Gleeson-White, *Double Entry: How the Merchants of Venice Created Modern Finance.* (Norton, 2013, pp. 92–97)

2 Milton Friedman, 'A Friedman doctrine – The Social Responsibility of Business is to Increase its Profits', *The New York Times Magazine*, 13 September, 1970.

Chapter 3: Accounting for the brain at work

1 Stephanie Cacioppo. *Wired for Love: A Neuroscientist's Journey Through Romance, Loss and the Essence of Human Connection.* (Robinson, 2022, p. 23)

2 Lara Boyd, *After watching this, your brain will not be the same*, TEDx Vancouver, December 2015. www.youtube.com/watch?v=LNHBMFCzznE

3 Katherine Woollett and Eleanor A. Maguire. *Acquiring 'the Knowledge' of London's Layout Drives Structural Brain Changes.* www.ncbi.nlm.nih.gov/pmc/articles/PMC3268356/ (last accessed 30 October, 2023)

4 Jo Hunter, Episode 134 Life Beyond the Numbers, *I Feel Like Me Again.*

5 Blakey Vermeule, *The New Unconscious: A Literary Guided Tour.* Chapter 22. *The Oxford Handbook of Cognitive Literary Studies*, Edited by Lisa Zunshine, pp. 464–482 (accessed via https://web.stanford.edu/~vermeule/cgi-bin/wp-content/uploads/2015/02/

unconscious-piece-proofs.pdf) (last accessed 1 November, 2023). This is referenced to Timothy D. Wilson, *Strangers to Ourselves: Discovering the Adaptive Unconscious.* (Belknap Press of Harvard University Press, 2004, p. 24)

[6] Lisa Feldman Barrett, *Seven and a Half Lessons About the Brain.* (Picador, 2020, p. 67)

[7] To gain a greater understanding on how concepts work read Lisa Feldman Barrett, *How Emotions Are Made: The Secret Life of the Brain.* (Pan Books, 2018)

[8] Lisa LLoyd, Episode 30 Life Beyond the Numbers, *Leading Change* and Episode 61, *Imagination.*

[9] This section on TPN and DMN is based on notes I took during *The Neuroscience of Change* course I attended in 2022 with Coaches Rising www.coachesrising.com/neuroscienceofchange/ The topic was presented by somatic leadership coach Amanda Blake during a pre-course workshop. She referenced the work of Professor Anthony Jack of Case Western Reserve University.

Chapter 4: Accounting for the body at work

[1] Kerry Cullen on Episode 127 of Life Beyond the Numbers, *The Performance Paradox.*

[2] Ana Bernardes on Episode 128 of Life Beyond the Numbers, *Alignment.*

[3] Amanda Blake, *The Neuroscience of Change* with Coaches Rising, 2022, and *Your Body is Your Brain: Leverage Your Somatic Intelligence to Find Purpose, Build Resilience, Deepen Relationships and Lead More Powerfully.* (Trokay Press, 2018)

[4] Nicholas Janni, *Leader as Healer: A New Paradigm for 21st Century Leadership.* (LID Publishing, 2022, p. 212)

5 Sue Rosen, Episode 143 of Life Beyond the Numbers, *Executive Presence.*

6 Peter Levine, *In an Unspoken Voice, How the Body Releases Trauma and Restores Goodness.* (North Atlantic Books, 2010, p. 11)

7 Deb Dana, *Anchored: How to Befriend Your Nervous System Using Polyvagal Theory.* (Sounds True, 2021, Chapter 5)

8 Steve Haines, episode 10 Life Beyond the Numbers, *This Feelings Business.*

9 The discussion on Polyvagal Theory was inspired and informed by the work of Deb Dana. Kerry Cullen, episode 127 *The Performance Paradox.*

10 Steve Haines, episode 10 Life Beyond the Numbers, *This Feelings Business.*

11 David Lee, episode 102 Life Beyond the Numbers, *Human Nature.*

12 For further exploration of Polyvagal Theory go to the Polyvagal Institute website www.polyvagalinstitute.org or Deb Dana's website www.rhythmofregulation.com

13 This is widely cited. Deb Dana, *Anchored: How to Befriend Your Nervous System Using Polyvagal Theory.* (Sounds True, 2021, p. 16)

14 Gavin Andrews, episode 38 Life Beyond the Numbers, *Wisdom & Technology.* Breathing techniques can be accessed on episode 40, *... and Breathe.* To learn more about the HeartMath Institute go to these websites www.heartmath.org and HeartMath www.heartmath.com

15 Giulia Enders, *Gut: The Inside Story of Our Body's Most Under-rated Organ.* (Scribe, 2016, p. 121)

Chapter 5: Reconciling brain, body and behaviour

1 *How We Feel* App: The How We Feel product team is led by Ben Silbermann, co-founder of Pinterest. The team includes current and former Pinterest employees who are passionate about creating a more emotionally healthy world. The scientific team is led by Dr. Marc Brackett and his team at the Yale University Center for Emotional Intelligence. https://howwefeel.org

2 Tiffany Watt Smith, *The Book of Human Emotions: An Encyclopaedia of Feeling from Anger to Wanderlust.* (Wellcome Collection, 2016, pp. 18–19)

3 https://feelthefeartraining.com/susan-jeffers-quotes-from-feel-the-fear-and-do-it-anyway/

4 Lisa Feldman Barrett, *How Emotions Are Made: The Secret Life of the Brain.* (Pan Books, 2018, p. 33)

5 David Whyte, *Consolations: The Solace, Nourishment and Meaning of Everyday Words.* (Canongate, 2019, p. 40)

6 Steve Haines, episode 10 Life Beyond the Numbers, *This Feelings Business.*

7 Steve Haines, *Anxiety is Really Strange.* (Singing Dragon, 2018, p. 27)

8 Professor Marc Brackett, *Permission to Feel: Unlock the Power of Emotions to Help Yourself and Your Child Thrive.* Part Two: The RULER Skills. (Quercus Editions Limited, 2019)

9 This was widely reported in newspapers at the time, and an internet search will generate a clip to watch.

Chapter 6: I'm only human: not rational or emotional but rational and emotional

[1] Greta Solomon, episode 80 Life Beyond the Numbers, *Why Do I Have to Fake it?*

[2] Eamon FitzGerald, episode 64 Life Beyond the Numbers, *Being Yourself.*

[3] Sue Rosen, episode 1 Life Beyond the Numbers, *Stepping Into the Unknown.*

[4] John Collins, episode 26, Life Beyond the Numbers, *Guinness & Tea.*

[5] Kris Lantheaume, Episode 111 Life Beyond the Numbers, *Success.*

Chapter 7: Accounting for emotions

[1] Lisa Feldman Barrett, *How Emotions Are Made: The Secret Life of the Brain.* (Pan Books, 2018, p. 178)

[2] Matthew Walker, *Why We Sleep: The New Science of Sleep and Dreams.* (Penguin Books, 2018, p. 137)

[3] Dr. Lara Boyd, *How Can Stress Affect Learning?* TEDxSurrey (6 July, 2022) www.youtube.com/watch?v=empLoDjYdrE

[4] There are a few variations of this definition. I obtained this one from World Health Organization Health and Wellbeing. www.who.int/data/gho/data/major-themes/health-and-well-being (last accessed 27 October, 2023)

[5] You can access this popular Yale University course *The Science of Wellbeing* on Coursera www.coursera.org

[6] Jim Loher and Tony Schwartz, *The Power of Full Engagement: Managing Energy, Not Time, Is the Key to High Performance and Personal Renewal.* (The Free Press, 2005, p. 31)

[7] World Health Organization physical activity key facts. www.who.int/news-room/fact-sheets/detail/physical-activity (last accessed 9 October, 2023)

[8] Steve Haines, episode 10 Life Beyond the Numbers, *This Feelings Business.*

[9] Professor Giana M. Eckhardt, episode 126 Life Beyond the Numbers, *Slowing Down.*

Chapter 8: Disintegration and dysregulation: regulation and integration

[1] Bernard Marr, *Key Performance Indicators: The 75 Measures Every Manager Needs to Know.* (Pearson, 2012, p. 270)

[2] www.adpri.org/research/global-workplace-study/

[3] www.rte.ie/archives/2016/0519/789560-sick-building-syndrome/

[4] Gib Bulloch, episode 28 Life Beyond the Numbers. *Breakthrough and The Intrapreneur: Confessions of a Corporate Insurgent.* (Unbound, 2018)

[5] U.S. Senate Committee on Commerce, Science and Transportation Aviation Safety Whistleblower Report under the leadership of Chair Maria Cantwell, December 2021 www.commerce.senate.gov/services/files/48E3E2DE-6DFC-4602-BADF-8926F551B670 (last accessed 16 October, 2023)

[6] Amy C. Edmondson Psychological Safety definition, TEDx video and The Fearless Scan questionnaire can all be found here https://amycedmondson.com/psychological-safety/

[7] See Google ReWork on teams at https://rework.withgoogle.com/ jp/subjects/teams You can go deeper into the results of the study in the NY Times article www.nytimes.com/2016/02/28/magazine/ what-google-learned-from-its-quest-to-build-the-perfect-team. html?smid=pl-share

[8] Douglas McGregor, *The Human Side of Enterprise,* Annotated Edition, updated with a new commentary by Joel Cutcher-Gershenfeld. (McGraw-Hill, 2006, p. 93)

[9] Ibid, p. 54.

[10] Ana Bernardes, episode 128 Life Beyond the Numbers, *Alignment.*

[11] I have seen and heard this description of trauma being credited to Gabor Mate multiple times on social media and websites – the closest I could find was 'Trauma is not what happens to us, but what we hold inside in the absence of an empathetic witness' in the Foreword to Peter Levine, *In an Unspoken Voice, How the Body Releases Trauma and Restores Goodness.* (North Atlantic Books, 2010, p. xii). You can also go to Dr Gabor Maté https:// drgabormate.com/the-wisdom-of-trauma/

[12] Kaveh Sadeghian, episode 51 Life Beyond the Numbers, *One to Many.* During our conversation Kaveh mentioned that Dr Sandra L. Bloom has done a tremendous amount of research on this and is moving into the organizational behaviour domain with her work – see www.creatingpresence.net

[13] Stephanie Cacioppo, PhD, *Wired for Love: A Neuroscientist's Journey Through Romance, Loss and the Essence of Human Connection.* (Robinson, 2022, p. 135)

[14] John Fairhurst, episode 124 Life Beyond the Numbers, *Facilitate People.*

[15] Nick Jemetta, episode 45 Life Beyond the Numbers, *Wellbeing Toolbox.*

[16] The IDGs are a work-in-progress and are being used beyond the SDGs space in businesses, communities and governments around the world. The IDG Framework is supported by Senior Scientific Advisors who are renowned academics and practitioners Amy C. Edmondson, Ph.D., Harvard Business School, Jennifer Garvey Berger, Ph.D., Harvard University Robert Kegan, Ph.D., Harvard University, Renée Lertzman, Ph.D., Cardiff University, Otto Scharmer, Senior Lecturer, MIT Sloan School of Management, Peter Senge, Senior Lecturer, MIT Sloan School of Management and Daniel J. Siegel, MD UCLA. For more see www.innerdevelopment-goals.org

[17] Katharina Moser, episode 132 Life Beyond the Numbers, *Inner Development Goals (IDGs).*

Chapter 9: Why doesn't everyone just get along – who is accountable and who is responsible?

[1] Matthew Phelan, *Freedom to be Happy: The Business Case for Happiness.* (H&H, 2020, pp. 82–83)

[2] Sheila Walsh, episode 27 Life Beyond the Numbers, *Healthy High Performance.*

[3] Matt Phelan, episode 67 Life Beyond the Numbers, *Better Understanding.*

[4] The authors are applying an insight of the late organizational culture theorist Edgar Schein, that organizational culture is present in the meeting room and the culture exists because people keep it alive. Peter Senge, C. Otto Scharmer, Joseph Jaworksi,

Betty Sue Flowers, *Presence Exploring Profound Change in People, Organizations and Society.* (Nicholas Brealey Publishing, 2006, pp. 48–50)

[5] Lie #8 Work–life balance matters most. Marcus Buckingham and Ashley Goodall, *Nine Lies About Work: A Freethinking Leaders Guide to the Real World.* (Harvard Business Review Press, 2019, pp. 181–205)

The bottom line: It's more than a feeling

[1] Aengus Fletcher, *The Science of Storytelling, Narrative and Creativity* appearing on Dr. Suzanne Evans' ChangeStories podcast https://changestories.libsyn.com/angus-fletcher-the-science-of-storytelling-narrative-and-creativity

[2] Rosamund Stone Zander, Benjamin Zander, *The Art of Possibility: Transforming Professional and Personal Life.* (Penguin Books, 2002)

[3] Matthew McConaghy Oscars acceptance speech www.youtube.com/watch?v=wD2cVhC-63I

[4] Jerry Harris, episode 9 Life Beyond the Numbers, *More than the Scorer.*

[5] Zoe Chance, *Influence is Your Superpower: How to Get What You Want Without Compromising Who You Are.* (Vermillion, 2022)

[6] Steven D'Souza and Diana Renner, *Not Knowing: The Art of Turning Uncertainty into Opportunity.* 2nd Edition. (LID Publishing Ltd, 2016, p. 224)

Bibliography and further resources

Barrett, Lisa Feldman. *How Emotions Are Made: The Secret Life of the Brain.* (Pan Books, 2018)

Barrett, Lisa Feldman. *Seven and a Half Lessons About the Brain.* (Picador, 2021)

Blake, Amanda. *Your Body is Your Brain: Leverage Your Somatic Intelligence to Find Purpose, Build Resilience, Deepen Relationships and Lead More Powerfully. (Trokay Press, 2018)*

Bond, Michael. *The Power of Others: Peer Pressure, Groupthink, and How the People Around Us Shape Everything We Do.* (Oneworld Publications, 2014)

Brackett, Marc. *Permission to Feel: Unlock the Power of Emotions to Help Yourself and Your Child Thrive.* (Quercus Editions Ltd, 2019)

Cacioppo, Stephanie. *Wired for Love: A Neuroscientist's Journey Through Romance, Loss and the Essence of Human Connection.* (Robinson, 2022)

Carlson, Neil R. *Physiology of Behaviour.* 10th Edition. (Allyn & Beacon, 2010)

Case, Helen Saul. *Orthomolecular Nutrition for Everyone: Megavitamins and Your Best Health Ever.* (Turner Publishing Company, 2017)

Chance, Zoe. *Influence Is Your Superpower: How to Get What You Want Without Compromising Who You Are.* (Vermillion, 2022)

Clear, James. *Atomic Habits: An Easy & Proven Way to Build Good Habits & Break Bad Ones.* (Random House Business Books, 2018)

Conley, Chip. *Emotional Equations: Simple Formulas to Help Your Life Work Better.* (Piatkus, 2013)

Covey, Stephen R. *The 7 Habits of Highly Effective People: Powerful Lessons in Personal Change.* (Simon & Schuster, 1999)

Dana, Deb. *Anchored: How to Befriend Your Nervous System Using Polyvagal Theory.* (Sounds True, 2021)

David, Susan. *Emotional Agility: Get Unstuck, Embrace Change, and Thrive in Work and Life.* (Penguin Life, 2017)

Davies, Stephanie. *Laughology: Improve Your Life with the Science of Laughter.* (Crown House Publishing Ltd, 2013)

Dent, Susie. *An Emotional Dictionary: Real Words for How You Feel from Angst to Zwodder.* (John Murray, 2022)

Deutsch, Bob with Lou Aronica. *The 5 Essentials: Using Your Inborn Resources to Create a Fulfilling Life.* (Hudson Street Press, 2013)

D'Souza, Steven and Diana Reiner. *Not Knowing: The Art of Turning Uncertainty into Opportunity.* 2nd edition. (LID Publishing Ltd, 2016)

Enders, Giulia. *Gut: The Inside Story of Our Body's Most Underrated Organ.* (Scribe, 2016)

Fosslien, Liz and Mollie West Duffy. *No Hard Feelings: Emotions at Work (and How They Help Us Succeed).* (Penguin Business, 2019)

Frankl, Viktor E. *Man's Search for Meaning: The Classic Tribute to Hope from the Holocaust.* (Rider, 2004)

Frazzetto, Giovanni. *How We Feel: What Science Can – and Can't – Tell Us About Our Emotions.* (Black Swan, 2014)

Gleeson-White, Jane. *Double Entry: How the Merchants of Venice Created Modern Finance.* (Norton, 2013)

Gleeson-White, Jane. *Six Capitals or Can Accountants Save The Planet? Rethinking Capitalism for the Twenty-First Century.* (Norton, 2015)

Goodall, Ashley and Marcus Buckingham. *Nine Lies About Work: A Freethinking Leader's Guide to the Real World.* (Harvard Business Review Press, 2019)

Gümüşay, Kübra. *Speaking and Being: How Language Binds and Frees Us.* (Profile Books, 2022)

Haines, Steve. *Anxiety is Really Strange.* (Singing Dragon, 2018)

Heath, Chip and Karla Starr. *Making Numbers Count: The Art and Science of Communicating Numbers.* (Bantam Press, 2022)

Heffernan, Margaret. *Beyond Measure: The Big Impact of Small Changes.* (TED Books, 2015)

Housel, Morgan. *The Psychology of Money: Timeless Lessons on Wealth, Greed, and Happiness.* (Harriman House, 2020)

Janni, Nicholas. *Leader as Healer: A New Paradigm for 21st Century Leadership.* (LID Publishing, 2022)

Jaworski, Joseph. *Synchronicity: The Inner Path of Leadership.* (Berrett-Koehler Publishers, 1996)

Jones, Alison. *Exploratory Writing: Everyday Magic for Life and Work.* (Practical Inspiration Publishing, 2023)

Keltner, Dacher. *Born to be Good: The Science of a Meaningful Life.* (Norton, 2009)

Kerr, James. *Legacy: What the All Blacks Can Teach Us About the Business of Life.* (Constable, 2020)

Keysers, Christian. *The Emphatic Brain: How the Discovery of Mirror Neurons Changes Our Understanding of Human Nature.* (Social Brain Press, 2011)

Lesser, Elizabeth. *Cassandra Speaks: When Women are the Storytellers, the Human Story Changes.* (HarperCollins, 2020)

Levine, Peter. *In an Unspoken Voice: How the Body Releases Trauma and Restores Goodness.* (North Atlantic Books, 2010)

Loher, Jim and Tony Schwartz. *The Power of Full Engagement: Managing Energy, Not Time, is the Key to High Performance and Personal Renewal.* (The Free Press, 2005)

Marr, Bernard. *Key Performance Indicators: The 75 Measures Every Manager Needs to Know.* (Pearson, 2012)

McGregor, Douglas. *The Human Side of Enterprise.* Annotated Edition. Updated and with new commentary by Joel Cutcher-Gershenfeld. (McGraw-Hill, 2006)

McLaren, Karla, M. (Ed.). *The Power of Emotions at Work: Accessing the Vital Intelligence in Your Workplace.* (Sounds True, 2021)

Mlodinow, Leonard. *Emotional: The New Thinking About Feelings.* (Allen Lane, 2022)

Neill, Michael. *The Inside-Out Revolution: The Only Thing You Need to Know to Change Your Life Forever.* (Hay House, 2013)

Neill, Michael. *The Space [Within]: Finding Your Way Back Home.* (Hay House, 2016)

Phelan, Matthew. *Freedom to be Happy: The Business Case for Happiness.* (Happiness and Humans Publishing, 2020)

Pink, Daniel H. *Drive: The Surprising Truth About What Motivates Us.* (Canongate Books, 2011)

Pink, Daniel H. *To Sell is Human: The Surprising Truth About Persuading, Convincing and Influencing Others.* (Canongate Books, 2018)

Senge, Peter, C., Otto Scharmer, Joseph Jaworski and Betty Sue Flowers. *Presence: Exploring Profound Change in People, Organizations, and Society.* (Nicholas Brealey Publishing, 2006)

Sinek, Simon. *Start with Why: How Great Leaders Inspire Everyone to Take Action.* (Portfolio Penguin, 2011)

Solomon, Greta. *Heart, Sass & Soul: Journal Your Way to Inspiration and Happiness.* (Mango, 2019)

Stone, Douglas, Bruce Patton and Sheila Heen. *Difficult Conversations: How to Discuss What Matters Most.* 10th Anniversary Edition. (Penguin, 2010)

Strozzi-Heckler, Richard. *The Art of Somatic Coaching: Embodying Skillful Action, Wisdom, and Compassion.* (North Atlantic Books, 2014) van der Kolk, Bessel. *The Body Keeps the Score: Mind, Brain and Body in the Transformation of Trauma*. (Penguin Books, 2015)

Walker, Matthew. *Why We Sleep: The New Science of Sleep and Dreams*. (Penguin Books, 2018)

Watt Smith, Tiffany. *The Book of Human Emotions: An Encyclopaedia of Feeling from Anger to Wanderlust*. (Profile Books, 2016)

Wax, Ruby, with a neuroscientist and a monk. *How to Be Human: The Manual*. (Penguin Life, 2018)

Whyte, David. *Consolations: The Solace, Nourishment and Underlying Meaning of Everyday Words*. (Canongate Books, 2019)

Zander, Rosamund Stone. *Pathways to Possibility: Transforming our Relationship with Ourselves, Each Other and the World*. (Penguin Books, 2017)

Zander, Rosamund Stone and Benjamin Zander. *The Art of Possibility: Transforming Professional and Personal Life*. (Penguin, 2002)

Websites

Accounting Made Easy: Gamified & Customised Finance for Non-Finance Managers Training. www.accountingmadeeasy.co

Center for Environmental Therapeutics: Automated Morn-ingness-Eveningness Questionnaire (AutoMEQ) for 'circa-dian rhythm type'. https://chronotype-self-test.info/index.php?newtest=Y&sid=61524

Coaches Rising. www.coachesrising.com

Dr Kristin Neff. Self-Compassion. https://self-compassion.org

Harvard Business Review. https://hbr.org

Lisa Feldman Barrett. https://lisafeldmanbarrett.com

MIT Sloan School of Management. https://mitsloan.mit.edu

Sounds True: The world's largest living library of transforma-tional teachings that support and accelerate spiritual awak-ening and personal transformation. www.soundstrue.com

The Evolving Leader Podcast. www.weareoutside.com/evolving-leader

The Happiness Index: The Employee Engagement and Happi-ness Platform. https://thehappinessindex.com

The Maslach Burnout Inventory. https://quiz.tryinteract.com/#/5ff8692ea989770016cbb2a0

The School of Life. At Work. Tools for Finding Fulfilling Work. www.theschooloflife.com/at-work/

Welltory Healthcare App. https://welltory.com

Acknowledgements

Creating or writing something might seem like a solitary endeavour and yet without other people this book would never have come into existence.

To all the people who sent their books into the world to both inform and inspire. I immersed myself in many of your wonderous works. The world is a better place because of your words.

Hosting a podcast is one of the most rewarding experiences of my work-life. Thank you to every person who has had a conversation with me on *Life Beyond the Numbers*. I learnt something in every conversation. And I am especially grateful to those of you whose contributions appear in this book.

It felt strange and scary to send my unfinished manuscript to people to read. Not only to read but also to invite them to tell me where they got bored or what they most enjoyed. So, from the bottom of my heart a huge thank you to Dee McMahon, Helen Joy, James Perry, James Rein, Kellie Lucas and Wilson Silva.

Steve Haines, I know that this book would never have been written if I had not met you. My gratitude can barely be expressed in words and is absolutely immeasurable.

Thanks to the many memorable mentors and coaches, who influenced me and helped me be a better version of myself. Those whom I worked with whose wisdom will never leave me include Mary Fulton, Mark Adams and John

Fairhurst. Clay Moffatt, you've helped me in so many ways and you have an uncanny ability of (re)appearing at exactly the right moment. Rob Lawrence you truly listened and furthered my creativity, curiosity and clarity. Kerry Cullen working with you, to begin close in, was a gift. Shay Nichols exploring sound and voice with you was as surprising as it was sacred. I am grateful to each and every one of you.

Thanks to my cohorts in *The Creative's Workshop (Pro7) and Ellev8 Masterpiece* for your camaraderie, challenges, encouragement and enlightenment. Thanks to my clients, friends, former colleagues and all in my global network who furthered my thinking.

I want to give a special shout out to my remarkable collaborator Helen Joy whose sense of humour is as infectious as her encouragement is unwavering. Our collaboration is meaningful to me and to those we serve. Helen your impact resonates through these pages.

Another special shout out to Kellie Lucas. Every time I phoned her, mostly when it was all getting to be *a bit too much*, she cut through the noise to get to the gold. Early in the writing process she gifted me a few days of her presence. I owe you a debt of gratitude Kellie.

There are people who are no longer alive but who live on in me. Thinking of them and indeed sensing them brought me comfort and courage – most especially Grandma, Uncle Tom, my sister Aoife and friend Billy Fitz. And to my late accountancy teacher, Liam Higgins, who encouraged a strength he saw in me that still pays dividends.

Thanks to my parents, Eilish and Ted, who instilled in me the resolve to be me. Thanks to my precious siblings, Alan and Siún, who always have my back. And to *Himself* who sees me and believes in me in a way that makes life better.

And finally, a wholehearted thank you to Alison Jones and the wider Practical Inspiration Publication team and community. I first met Alison in 2020 and her encouragement, energy, enthusiasm and practical approach continue to inspire.

About the author

Susan Ní Chríodáin, founder of consultancy Beyond the Numbers, is on a mission to revolutionize workplaces. An award-winning chartered accountant hailing from the Big 4, her career spans three continents and a range of diverse leadership positions.

From navigating international crises to reshaping organizational culture, she brings a unique blend of resilience, empathy and business acumen to the table. But it is her gift for connecting at a deeper level that sets her apart.

Today, based in the UK, she advocates for creating workplaces where everyone can bring their best selves to work, bridging the gap between organizational performance and personal well-being. With a blend of Irish wit and worldly wisdom, Susan is more than a consultant – she's your guide to unlocking the full potential of your organization.

A lifelong learner, Susan's curiosity knows no bounds. Whether she's delving into the depths of organizational dynamics or exploring existentialism, she's always seeking fresh perspectives.

A lover of the sea, books and CrossFit, Susan's zest for life infuses her work. Her popular podcast, Life Beyond the Numbers, invites listeners to discover insights on how to have a more fulfilling work-life.

Find out more by visiting www.beyond-thenumbers.com

Index

A quick word from Practical Inspiration Publishing...

We hope you found this book both practical and inspiring – that's what we aim for with every book we publish.

We publish titles on topics ranging from leadership, entrepreneurship, HR and marketing to self-development and wellbeing.

Find details of all our books at: www.practicalinspiration.com

 **Did you know...**

We can offer discounts on bulk sales of all our titles – ideal if you want to use them for training purposes, corporate giveaways or simply because you feel these ideas deserve to be shared with your network.

We can even produce bespoke versions of our books, for example with your organization's logo and/or a tailored foreword.

To discuss further, contact us on info@practicalinspiration.com.

 Got an idea for a business book?

We may be able to help. Find out more about publishing in partnership with us at: bit.ly/PIpublishing.

Follow us on social media...

🐦 @PIPTalking

📷 @pip_talking

📘 @practicalinspiration

♪ @piptalking

in Practical Inspiration Publishing